SERMONS
Preached at Harvard

SERMONS
Preached at Harvard

by
WILLARD L. SPERRY

**Dean Emeritus of the Harvard Divinity School
and former Chairman of the Board of Preachers
to the University**

Harper & Brothers, Publishers, New York

'53

TO
MURIEL B. SPERRY
MY FAVORITE CRITIC,
GENEROUS, JUST AND ALWAYS AFFECTIONATE

CONTENTS

Contents

FOREWORD

THESE sermons have all been preached at Sunday services in the Memorial Church at Harvard, i.e. our University "college chapel."

They cover a period of ten years, from 1943 to 1953. Their background is, therefore, World War II and the inconclusive peace which has followed that war. They presuppose the still unsettled state of our world and the consequent perplexities in the lives of individuals. They do not labor this point; they accept it as a premise.

I find, as I have moved around our colleges over these years, that wherever one goes the student mind is more or less uniform. Youth is not finding it easy to say that life and the world are indubitably good. Neither does youth say that they are hopelessly evil. The somber dread is that human life may be merely meaningless. Youth is fortified in this suspicion by some of the more sophisticated philosophies of our time, as expressed in drama, fiction, secular existentialism and the like. Many, if not most, of these sermons have been consciously or unconsciously addressed to this widespread skepticism in college circles.

In one of his famous sonnets George Meredith says,

Ah, what a dusty answer gets the soul,
When hot for certainties in this our life.

9

Superficially college life is by no means a matter of low spirits.
There is among undergraduates today, as there always has
been, gaiety and genuine intellectual interest. Youth is much
too vital to be depressed. In particular, the zest of thought
in the areas of the natural sciences is sustained by the bewil-
dering and amazing discoveries being made within their specialized areas.

It is said that it is the task of the sciences to ask the question "How?" and of the humanities to ask the question "Why?"

A wholly laudable and defensible attempt to answer the
first of these questions may and often does absorb the modern
mind. But behind preoccupation with exciting answers to that
question lies the suspicion that the second question "Why?"
cannot be answered, therefore it is not worth while to waste
time asking it. This suspicion on the part of the student is fortified by the indifference of many scientists on a faculty to the
humanities, and by their studied agnosticism in the whole area
of religion. How often does one of them say or seem to imply,
"That is not my field."

The secularization of American higher education has gone
very far, and is, given modern specialization, academically defensible. The old theological answers to the question "Why?"
are no longer compatible with much of our modern knowledge.
One of the most familiar figures on the American campus is
the mature and distinguished professor who had been brought
up as a child and youth within the brutal strait jacket of a now
incredible creed. He has with great effort escaped from one
or another of those strait jackets and is determined never again
to let himself be caught in a similar situation, however liberal

and modernistic its terms. One can sympathize with these persons. But, since the question "Why?" is in some ways ultimately more important than the question "How?" such faculty members leave their students unhelped in the area of life where help is most needed.

These sermons, therefore, are in the first instance a challenge to the student to go on asking the question "Why?" even though they hazard no single dogmatic answer to that immediate and absorbing problem. Such answers as are ventured here still fall, I hope, within the broad area of our historic Christian faith. They are not, however, briefs for any particular dogmas, whether to the theological right or the left. Their very neutrality, which is implicit in the conception of a nonsectarian college chapel, may be a theological weakness. But I have never had any desire to "convert" any parishioner, whether in a church or college chapel, to my own private religious convictions. Rather I have been concerned to make him realize that, ultimately, the question "Why?" is all-important and to encourage him to go on asking that question and to try to find his own answer.

Although these sermons were written and delivered with students in mind they were not intended to exclude the older members of the congregation. Any man who has left normal parish work and taken over the conduct of a college chapel feels that to a certain extent his horizons have been narrowed. In preaching to college students one is always aware that their range of experience falls short of the total content of man's threescore years and ten. One is speaking on the spot and at the time to a somewhat limited cross section of human life.

The adulation of children is a common and sometimes rather trying phase of American life. So, also, the flattery of the undergraduate. Our college students are probably the most alert and important group in the community, since the future is going to depend more upon them than upon any other single unit in society. They will make the mind of the church and state of tomorrow. But they should come up to their future humbly, not thinking of themselves more highly than they ought to think. Therefore, sermons in college chapels probably ought not to be confined to the immediate preoccupations of undergraduate life. Many of us, over years of college preaching, have concluded that a sermon which seems to have served the needs of hearers in a parish church is more likely to be helpful to students than a sermon which confines itself strictly to their immediate interests.

WILLARD L. SPERRY

Cambridge, Massachusetts

SERMONS
Preached at Harvard

I

THE MIND OF CHRIST

Text: Let this mind be in you, which was also in Christ Jesus.
PHILIPPIANS 2:5

CHRISTIANITY is often spoken of as one of the world's great "book religions." Not only is the Bible a great book but it has prompted thousands of other books. It is generally agreed that, after we leave the Bible, the medieval work of devotion called *The Imitation of Christ* has been the most widely read and influential of all Christian books.

It is a fair question whether that title was ever intended by the author. It happens to be merely the title of the first chapter of the first section of his work. Beyond that literary accident there is the further and more serious question whether the life described in the book and proposed as the Christian ideal has the slightest correspondence to the life of Jesus. Many Protestants have dismissed the *Imitation* as "a manual of sacred selfishness." There is, I think, no doubt that Francis of Assisi was a more accurate and successful imitator of Jesus than was Thomas á Kempis.

15

Then there is the further and still more pertinent question as to whether trying to be a Christian ever ought to be a matter of imitating Jesus. One of the great church historians, Adolf Harnack, says that this whole idea of the Imitation of Christ appeared only very late in time and then at a time when Christianity seemed to have lost its vital originality and initiative. The best it could do was to try to live a secondhand life. We occasionally see these would-be modern imitators of Christ on the streets of our cities; long curling hair, a white seamless robe, sandals on their dusty feet. It is a fair question whether imitation of that literal sort has anything to do with the Christian religion, or was, indeed, ever intended and anticipated by Jesus himself.

We are, therefore, probably on safer ground when we avoid too literal imitation of the life of Christ and try to relate ourselves to him in some other way. For instance, we cannot do better than to turn to the words of the text in one of Paul's letters, "Let this mind be in you, which was also in Christ Jesus." One of our modern translations is undoubtedly nearer the mark, "Have the same attitude that Christ Jesus had" (Goodspeed).

There are three somewhat interrelated words which, in this connection, ought to be distinguished: the words "pose," "position" and "attitude." A pose is an affectation, not a transcript of the true nature of the poseur. We all know the social poseurs, the political poseurs, the aesthetic poseurs, the academic poseurs. And there are, also, the familiar religious poseurs, sometimes in important church offices. We do not and cannot take any of them very seriously.

The word "position" is a more serious term. It represents a fixed conviction on which a man takes his stand and from which he will not be dislodged. So, Martin Luther at the Diet of Worms said, "Here I stand, God help me, I can do nought else." It is a common term in warfare. Your position must be held at all costs. And there are certain desperate moral situations which can be dealt with only in those terms. But in general the word "position" seems somewhat rather static and immobile. In any case, this word is, for the uses of religion, a curiously lifeless one. I may ask you what position you hold on episcopal ordination, or the baptism of infants, or the use of sacraments. But my question will be a matter of curiosity. I know I cannot dislodge you from your position, and I get little personal help from your inflexibility in matters of faith and practice.

So we come to the word "attitude." Athletes often pose for a photographer, but that is not the same thing as the alert attitude they take when they are on the mark waiting for the gun. So it is with the kind of world most of us know best. The photographer will pose us and ask us to keep the pose, while he takes the picture, but we know that the result is not the transcript of a real attitude.

It is today far more important to try to understand what is meant by the phrase the "attitude that was in Christ Jesus" than to strike a Christian pose or even to hold a Christian position. The word "attitude" always implies action as its consequence. To try to understand, by reading the Gospels over and over again, what the attitude of Jesus was toward life and the world, God and his fellow men, is a far better lead for the difficult task of trying to be a Christian than to affect a formal imitation of Christ, a studied Christian pose, a static affirmation of a Christian position.

May I hazard then three or four brief suggestions as to what may be meant by the injunction, "Have the same attitude that Christ Jesus had."

The words seem to suggest that Christianity is a matter of method, mental and moral method, quite as much as a matter of results. In this respect might we say that science has a good deal to teach religion. If the method is not trustworthy we cannot place any confidence in its conclusions. Some of you know the name of Charles Péguy, a brilliant young French writer, who died at the head of his company in the First Battle of the Marne. His biographer said of him that he always invited his readers to eat in the kitchen, that he wanted them to share not merely in consuming the meal, but to share also in the preparation of the meal. The great historic religions of the authoritative kind invite us to eat their finished meal in the dining room; the less formal religions, which most of us know best, invite us to eat in the kitchen, that is, to share and have confidence in their method. May something of that sort be meant by the Gospel statement that Jesus is our Way, as well as our destination. That seems to have been his attitude.

The jeering crowds at the foot of the cross said that he "trusted in God." Nothing that could have been said then or that can be said now is more accurate. This was Christ's most native attitude toward life and the world. In the end it is what every religious person has to do. He cannot rationally justify his act in advance. Knowledge cannot prove that he is warranted in this act. Christ never disparaged nor discouraged our own human efforts after righteousness, but he also trusted implicitly in what Matthew Arnold called a "power not ourselves that makes for righteousness," and to that power he gave the name of God his Father. If we are not willing to relax ourselves, to let ourselves go in some such act of trust, it is hard to see how we can share Christ's attitude. Too great caution and timidity, too critical and skeptical an approach to life make religion difficult to understand and experience.

Christ trusted his fellow men. It is true that his trust was sometimes betrayed. He chose Judas Iscariot as one of the twelve and Judas failed him. If the truth of Judas be the one commonly accepted that he was a selfish and treacherous man, then Jesus made a mistake in the initial choice. In any case Jesus erred on the side of confidence in men. Most of us are imperfectly Christian in that respect today. We err on the side of caution in dealing with others. This habit has been fostered in us by the disappointments and disillusionments in the history of our own time. To discover that solemn compacts are dismissed as scraps of paper, that acceptance of acts of appeasement is merely a matter of being shown up as incompetent fools—these experiences have sobered our native trust in humanity. It is worth adding that what is imperiled today is not merely the traditional Christian attitude toward man, but the sober democratic and liberal appraisal of man. It may be that both are unwarranted and mistaken. But increasingly one has the feeling that we are probably erring on the wrong side in this matter.

Christ's attitude toward the organized life of man presupposed the one idea which was always uppermost in his mind and to which all other ideas were oriented, that of the Kingdom of Heaven. There are two terms which are commonly used to describe society so organized: one is the Kingdom of God, the other is the Church. In most European countries the idea of the Church is the familiar one. Our forefathers came out here to found what they called a "Holy Commonwealth," that is, the Kingdom of God as they construed it. In general the thought of the Kingdom of God has been more to the front of the American mind than that of the Church. It has been only as society as a whole seems to have fallen short of the brave dream of our Founding Fathers that we have been emphasizing the Church. The native attitude of the mind of Christ anticipated the whole of human life organized under God. It will be a serious interruption of our Christian tradition if we abandon that ideal and take refuge in some more restricted vision for human society.

And finally Jesus' attitude toward life itself and the principle of life was confident. He came that we might have life and have it abundantly. The profound ascetic distrust of life which is found in so many religions, philosophies and ethical systems is simply no part of the mind of Christ. Discipline, yes; but distrust, no. That is why the observance of Easter is felt to be in character, not out of character. There are many modern cults which fit the discouraging times in which we have been living which have parted company with the attitude of Christ Jesus. There is, perhaps, no point at which we more need the mind that was in Christ Jesus.

II

THE NATURE OF FAITH

Text: When the Son of man cometh, shall he find faith on the earth?—LUKE 18:8

WHEN John Woolman was preaching to the Indians in Western Pennsylvania he had an Indian interpreter who translated for him. The Indian said to him one day, "I love to feel where words come from."

Most of us share that loving curiosity. The older we grow and the more we think about things, the greater the fascination of words. We never really master their elusive mystery. We become aware of that elusive quality, as did Woolman's interpreter, when we try to translate from one language to another.

We have all seen notices of the publication of the Revised Standard Version of the Bible, at which a committee of American scholars had been working for some fifteen or twenty years. If we were to ask any member of the revision committee what had been their hardest problem he would certainly tell us that it had constantly arisen from the fact that there is no precise English equivalent for many words in the Hebrew and Greek originals.

Even when we confine ourselves to our own language the great words of the language are hard to track down to their true meaning. The trouble is that they are many-sided, and no one definition comes anywhere near telling the whole truth about them. In his chapter on "Mountains" in *Modern Painters* Ruskin had a set of drawings of the Matterhorn. The most familiar is that of the Matterhorn as seen from Zermatt, an abrupt and towering pyramid. But seen from the western side or from the farther Italian slopes the Matterhorn is a rather gentle and gradually sloping mountain. So it is with words. We may tunnel through the base of a great word and come out on the far side. But by so doing we have learned little about it. The best we can do is to move around its base and look at it from many angles.

Here, then, is this many-sided word "faith." It is a word upon which religion rests and in want of it there is no possibility of understanding what religion is. Within religion it is the antithesis to the word "works." Works are religion in action, busied with practical service of others. Faith is the motive for these acts of humble and unselfish service. It is the secret of the strength by which we carry out those works. It is our reason for doing them. Every religion is concerned with what is traditionally called "the contemplative life" and the "active life." No religion has ever agreed, and no religious persons have ever agreed as to which is the more important. There are the Sons of Mary and the Sons of Martha. Most of us know, individually, which kind of a son we temperamentally are. And most of us are aware of the need of self-correction in this matter, a deliberate cultivation of the opposite point of view. So, also, the word "faith" differentiates religion from science. In science we know or try to know—to reach intellectual certainty. In religion we believe. The main difference is that religion is mainly and most characteristically concerned with all that lies beyond the areas of our knowledge. It is often said that we are under no bonds to concern ourselves with those marginal and mysterious areas of reality, but such a statement ignores the fact that our attitude toward these mysteries sets the whole tone of life.

Pilate's wife came to him at the time of the trial of Jesus and said, "Have thou nothing to do with that just man." A great many prudent persons propose or affect that procedure in the presence of the marginal mysteries of life, which are the areas that can be occupied only by faith. The difficulty is that once we have become aware of these mysteries, they will not let us alone. We may keep them at a kind of mental arm's length, but they are always breaking through our guard.

What do we mean, then, by faith? The Bible seems to me to suggest a half dozen different meanings, and I venture to mention four of them briefly so that we may perhaps better understand that poignant cry, "When the Son of man cometh, shall he find faith on the earth?"

In the final books of the New Testament the word has come to have a rather conventional meaning. Thus, St. Paul says, "I have kept the faith." The latter epistles talk about "the faith once delivered to the saints." So used the word presupposes a formulated set of ideas which have become a crystallized tradition. For many persons this is, perhaps, the most familiar meaning of the word. Faith is continuing acceptance of the articles of belief of one's church. Of all meanings of the word this is, on the whole, the most limited and mechanical. If it were not for the heretics and come-outers who have broken the faith, so construed, rather than kept it, we should still be shackled to ancient and now incredible ideas. But I venture to suggest that the word "tradition," and faith in this connection implies a tradition, does not presuppose a static world of ideas. A tradition is a living and moving thing. It is in motion and it has what the sailors call steerage way. A becalmed tradition is not really a tradition. A tradition implies a continuity of inner life. To break with tradition, in this sense of the word, is psychologically a very dangerous procedure. As Christians most of us today do not want to break with the tradition of our religion. We must keep moving; we want to carry on. So construed we are well advised to "keep the faith."

The eleventh chapter of the Epistle to the Hebrews comes at the word from quite another angle. "Faith," it announces, "is the substance of things hoped for, the evidence of things not seen."

Of all possible meanings of the word this is in some ways the most intelligible to our kind of world. Faith is an adventure or better still the verification of a hypothesis. It is an exploration of the unknown, an attempt to prove a theory. His faith was for Columbus not merely the vague idea that there must be land to the West; it was his act as well. All of our pioneer experiments in science are acts of faith. Edison had an idea that an incandescent electric bulb ought to be possible.

How many experiments did he make before he proved his theory? It was many hundreds. So construed we live in a world which is prompted and sustained by faith. Faith is the giving of substance to what seems in advance to be plausible, even possible. That definition holds good in the imponderable realm with which human relations are concerned as well as with the ponderables of science. Getting married is and always must be a tremendous venture of faith. There is absolutely no way of proving scientifically in advance that there is warrant for the deeply felt emotion of love and that this emotion will stand the wear and tear of a lifetime. So in religion, with its bold hypotheses, the Bible says that he who doeth the will, and presumably only he who doeth the will, shall know the doctrine. Are the Christian virtues defensible? The only way one can satisfy oneself on a simple and elemental question like this is to go ahead and try them. Bernard Shaw divided society into two groups, the occupants of Heartbreak House and those of Horseback Hall. The former were the so-called intellectuals; the latter the hard-bitten men of action. He said that if he had to live with one group rather than the other he would choose the occupants of Horseback Hall, because those who lived in Heartbreak House never intend to do anything about the ideas they hold. So a modern philosopher has said that all thought is action in suspense. But until thought, particularly the kind of thought with which religion is concerned, is crystallized or precipitated in action, faith is meaningless. I suppose that is what the Epistle of James means when it says, "Faith without works is dead." Religion is something more than a perpetual discussion group.

For St. Paul the word "faith" had another and a unique

meaning. Paul's faith had a single object, and that object was Christ. When he said that he believed, he was thinking of his single-minded personal devotion to Christ. In one way or another this has been the most characteristic form of Christian faith. This faith has sometimes taken the form of a mystical identification with Christ, in which the disciple feels himself actually one with Christ. It is not the disciple who lives and acts; it is Christ within him. And even for those of us who have never had mystical experiences Washington Gladden's hymn, "O Master, let me walk with thee," is very near to what we mean by believing in Christ.

Some years ago Richard Watson Gilder wrote two stanzas which he attributed to a heathen sojourning in Galilee in the year A.D. 32. Presumably this heathen had seen the crucifixion and shared the experiences of the disciples on Easter. In any case the heathen says,

> If Jesus Christ is a man—
>   and only a man,—I say
> That of all mankind I cleave to him,
>   And to him will I cleave alway.
>
> If Jesus Christ is a God—
>   And the only God,—I swear
> I will follow him through heaven and hell,
>   The earth, the sea, the air!

This is what our Quaker poet meant when he said,

> O Lord, and Master of us all!
>   Whate'er our name or sign,
> We own Thy sway, we hear Thy call,
>   We test our lives by Thine.

In the final paragraph of his great book, *The Quest of the Historical Jesus,* Schweitzer says that Jesus comes to us today as a man without a name, unknown. But to those who follow him he will reveal himself and in their own experience they shall know who he is. Christian faith always must be an attempt, in our own experience, to give substance to our idea of Christ.

And, then, there is finally the idea of faith in the Gospels, and in the mind and life of Jesus himself. It is hard to know just what faith meant to Jesus. But is seems to mean, above all else, the willingness to relax the strain of moral effort and to trust in God. It is like learning to swim. As long as you struggle to keep afloat you are in danger of sinking. It is only when you realize that if you will let yourself go the element around you will itself keep you up.

Most of us have had and all of us will have this experience of daring to give up trying to be self-sufficient. The moral struggle is important but it is not the whole of life. There is also this ultimate willingness to relax, just to let ourselves go and trust the world of the spirit to bear us up. There is no advance proof that it will do so, yet when one puts this faith that it will do so to the test, there comes a curious quiet and confidence. Faith, as Jesus thought and spoke of it, seems to have been just that utter relaxation. The mockers at the foot of the cross said, "He trusted in God." The word that was spoken in jest was the truth of Jesus. I know of no writer, ancient or modern, who has come nearer to the theory and practice of faith in the person of Jesus, than our own New England poet Whittier. In this matter he is more true to the

mind of Christ than most of the thousands of theologians who
have tried to pluck the secret out of the Gospels. Any one of the
possible interpretations of faith which we have suggested is
plausible and defensible and helpful. In the end it seems to
come down to our trustful relaxation and restfulness in our
thought of God. Here is the great repose of our religion.

> O brothers! if my faith is vain,
>   If hopes like these betray,
> Pray for me that my feet may gain
>   The sure and safer way.
>
> And Thou, O Lord! by whom are seen
>   Thy creatures as they be,
> Forgive me if too close I lean
>   My human heart on Thee!

III

THE DESIRE OF DISCIPLINE

Text: The very true beginning of [wisdom] is the desire of discipline.—WISDOM OF SOLOMON 6:17

WE Americans have, or like to think we have, a great many good points. In a world where most people are reduced to naked poverty we are still relatively rich. In a world where countless persons have lost hope for themselves and their children we have hope for our future. We are a kindly people at heart. There is in this country today a vast reservoir of untapped sympathy for starving folks in Europe and Asia. It needs only to find an adequate official outlet. At a time when some states have given up all sense of formal obligation to God we maintain our traditional faith in religion. We are not a godless nation. All these things are true of us.

But we have one serious national fault. We are an undisciplined people. Indeed, we seem to have turned our lack of discipline into a kind of perverse virtue, of which we are secretly proud.

Why this should be so is a cultural and moral riddle. Our lack of self-discipline may be a misinterpretation of the idea of America as the land of liberty. For three hundred years immigrants have been coming here to escape from harsh oppression in the Old World. The Land of Promise has always seemed to such persons a place where one may do as one likes.

Or once again our lack of discipline may be a hangover from the days of the frontier. American scholars are now generally agreed that the frontier is the passkey to our whole national history. A frontier is a lawless place. There may be, there probably is, a residual frontiersman in every one of us.

If any solution to the problem is to be found it will have to come from our churches on the one hand, and our schools and colleges on the other hand.

The Old Testament has a word for the cure. It is the word "Wisdom." As most of us know, it took a thousand years to write the Old Testament. The earliest writers were primitive poets who wrote songs of battle. Then came storytellers, prophets, historians, lawgivers, priests. Last of all came the wise men of Israel, who gave us what is called the "Wisdom Literature" of the Old Testament.

No single simple definition has ever been found for the word "Wisdom," either as it was used then, or as we use it now. In the book of Proverbs it meant reverence for God and therefore for the law of God. In the modern world it means, according to Webster, the "ability to judge soundly and deal sagaciously with facts, especially as they relate to life and conduct." The word is, therefore, concerned with some kind of thinking which is more than information or specialized skills. These may be its presuppositions, but they do not exhaust it. Specialized knowledge has given us in these last years a staggering number of discoveries as to possible ways of making war more deadly, but it is left to wisdom to try to decide what shall be done with these discoveries hereafter now that we have them.

Wisdom implies, therefore, a certain maturity of mind. If it can be called a skill, its skill concerns the total conduct of life. It means learning how to live with oneself and with other people. It means that, having made peace with oneself, one can keep the peace with other men. It means that, for oneself, one has decided what really matters in this life, as against things that matter little or not at all.

It is a matter of common report, so common that it is now a truism, that in the modern world our specialized skills have outrun our total wisdom. This proposition has been a platitude for the last twenty or thirty years, but that does not mean that it is not true.

Let us assume that what the world needs today is more wisdom, and that therefore we ought to be trying to become wise men. How then do we set about it?

Well, the text of the morning gives us the answer, "The *very beginning* of [wisdom] is the desire of discipline."

We are starting another college year. Those students who have not yet got the feel of this University may have heard by report what they will eventually discover by experience, that Harvard is trying to pull the process of instruction together into some dominant type of transaction, which shall bring our wisdom abreast our skills. This venture, listed as "general education," is not an easy task. The whole procedure is still a matter of trial and error. Some students may have to be its guinea pigs. But if they will accept that lot, they will have the satisfaction of knowing that they are sharing in what is perhaps the most needed venture in our whole American educational life.

Now one cannot take part in this venture, or hope to profit by what the University is trying to do, unless one has from the start what the text calls this "desire of discipline."

This desire does not always come easily or naturally. When I was a boy I had a saddle pony. He was often running loose at pasture. To get a halter or bridle on him was a tricky business. He would let you within a foot of him, then turn and kick up his heels and be off down the field. He would nibble cautiously at a pan of oats which I held in one hand, but he always had a wary eye for the bridle held in the other hand behind my back. This game went on for half an hour, until on his own account he would trot right up to be bridled and saddled. I always liked him for his playfulness, and there ought to be in all of us something of that native independence. We should not sell our freedom too soon or too easily.

On the other hand all of us, in our wiser moments, realize that most of the enduring of life comes from a willing acceptance of discipline. Thus, an Oxford philosopher, the late R. G. Collingwood, has said that all that is meant by philosophy begins in games. The common quality of all games is this, that they are played inside a field and within rules. It is said that the game of lacrosse was invented by the American Indians in the northwest, and that as first played, the man with the ball in his crosse might run from the Mississippi River to the Pacific Coast. So played it was not a true game or a good game. There must be the chalk lines. Play stops when one gets out of bounds or when one breaks the rules. Every athelete knows what is meant by the necessary acceptance of the playing field and the rule book; indeed if he is to become a first-rate athlete he will be prompted by a genuine desire of discipline. And that is why, out in the world, a good athlete is often a wiser man than a specialized pedant.

Or take one more area of life: what we mean and all that we mean by the arts. Once again the common trait in all arts is the acceptance of a principle of pattern. There is no such thing as a wholly unpatterned art. The most difficult piece of English to write is, probably, the sonnet. Its pattern is rigid and universally recognized. There are fourteen lines; three quatrains and a final couplet. The meter is five-foot iambics. The rhyme allows only the slightest variations. Thus Wordsworth, in describing the work of his great predecessor Milton, speaks of "the sonnet's scanty plot of ground." Nothing could be more accurate. Yet when a master like Shakespeare or Milton or Wordsworth writes a sonnet he has done the most difficult, the most skillful, and what is more important, the most successful thing that words allow.

This University, therefore, is going to provide its students with certain mental patterns, to be used in the interpretation of nature and history and one's own life. Whatever the final truthfulness of any one of the patterns, the principle of pattern will obtain. At their best these patterns aim at wisdom.

And there is for every one of us, whether teacher or student, the initial personal question, Am I still irked by the discipline which the principle of pattern requires, or can I honestly say that I am moved by that desire of discipline which is the very true beginning of wisdom?

The problem in the general area of morals and religion is not radically different. A World War II chaplain back from four years in the Pacific said that the average American G.I. was not interested in religion, because he thought religion was merely the sum of the things one might not do. It was a set of prohibitions and negations. There is nothing new in that account of the matter. Chaplains in World War I brought back just the same report.

Well, there is some warrant for this idea. The very word "religion" means a binding order, a set of regulations to be accepted and obeyed. Men who are chronically undisciplined will not like the idea of religion, but that is not necessarily a condemnation of religion itself.

One of the oldest and most rigid moral patterns in the world is the Ten Commandments. They are negative and prohibitory. There is no getting away from it. Most of them begin, "Thou shalt not." But it is a fairly serious business to ignore the Ten Commandments, and as someone once remarked, "If you want to find out what they are all about, just break one of them."

It is commonly said that Christianity is positive, whereas Judaism was negative, and therefore that it ought to be easier to be a Christian. There is, indeed, much ground for this statement. One of the simplest and most comprehensive accounts of Christianity is St. Augustine's daring and splendid statement, "Love, and do what you like." It is, however, very easy to go on from that permissive rule for life to the conclusion that Christianity is merely a matter of doing what you like, irrespective of the love which conditions your liking. But in their own way the Beatitudes and the thirteenth chapter of I Corinthians are just as rigid patterns for living as the Commandments. Indeed, they are more rigid.

Read St. Paul's passage in the latest revised translation. "Love is patient and kind; love is not jealous or boastful; it is not arrogant or rude; love does not insist on its own way, it is not irritable or resentful." If we really have these tempers we may safely do as we like, but doing as we like in want of them cannot be called Christianity. One might say of St. Paul's chapter on love what Wordsworth said of Milton's sonnets, that at first it seems a "scanty plot of ground." In any case it is a formal pattern for the fashioning of character; it is not a brief for unpatterned living.

The trouble with most of us is that we are still morally so undisciplined that we have not come to the point where we desire the kind of rigorous discipline that the Beatitudes and the chapter on love ask of us. Yet here is the warrant for moral and spiritual wisdom. Only as we accept the principle of pattern and the necessity for the discipline which every pattern requires shall we become persons with whom the Christian tempers are matters of second mental nature.

We are told that in times of crisis and opportunity our conduct is seldom determined by our surface conscious thought. The whole deeper stuff of the mind takes control then. The yield of our accumulated living over the years decides what we shall do at such times. Here, then, is the ground for those patient constant disciplines in Christian living which at times seem so mechanical and other times so dull; reading the Bible, going to church, saying our prayers. It is out of these habits that wisdom is matured, slowly but certainly. And the beginning of wisdom is a genuine desire of moral and spiritual discipline.

If one does not realize this in advance, then one can only hope, as the wise man of Israel said long ago, that "wisdom will torment you with her discipline, until she may trust your soul."

IV

LARGER IDEAS OF GOD

Text: For the bed is shorter than that a man can stretch himself on it: and the covering narrower than that he can wrap himself in it.—ISAIAH 28:20

THE Bible is a serious book. It is not, however, a solemn book. Since it is a serious, but not a solemn book, it makes occasional use of humor. Solemn people do not or cannot laugh. Serious people can laugh and do laugh at the right time and on the right occasion.

No one has studied carefully the place of humor in religion. It plays a rather minor part, but from time to time an important part. One might say that a Christian does not laugh too long and too loudly at other people, but that now and then he ought to laugh at himself. For laughter has in certain situations an antiseptic quality not matched by any other act or attitude.

Such laughter usually takes the form of irony. Irony is a powerful moral agent and ought to be used cautiously, otherwise it becomes the crackling of thorns under a pot, mere cynicism. But when used properly ironic humor can destroy the sham solemnities of life and restore to us a sense of its serious realities. Thus, there is no little ironic humor in the teaching of Jesus. though we are so familiar with his words that we have lost our feeling for their preposterousness. Take, for instance, his words about swallowing a camel, but choking at a gnat; or, again, worrying about the speck of dust in your neighbor's eye, but ignoring the two by four in your own eye.

Of all the bits of irony in the Bible, that of the text is one of the most picturesque and suggestive. The prophet is asking himself and his people, What is the matter with our religion? And he replies, Our religion is not long enough to accommodate the facts or broad enough to cover the facts. Our religion is too meager for the world we are now living in. "The bed is shorter than that a man can stretch himself on it: and the covering narrower than that he can wrap himself in it." If one has ever spent a night on a bed like that, with blankets like that, this homely metaphor needs no further explanation.

The Bible is, in no small part, an attempt to find longer beds and wider blankets to cover the cold facts. The first Psalm, for instance, says that the godly man will always prosper and the ungodly shall be like chaff which the wind drives away. In the long run this may be so. Goodness certainly has a longer expectation of life than badness, but this proposition cannot always be proved in the experience and lifetime of a single individual. The book of Job is nothing but story of the effort of a good man to understand the meaning of his own un-deserved sufferings. The facts gave the lie to the doctrines; religiously he was out in the cold.

Much of the loss of religion, as that process is popularly described, comes from the futile attempt to make old dogmas cover facts which have outgrown them. We cannot deny the facts; as Huxley says, we have to bow down before facts like a little child and go wherever they lead. That is one of the contributions which science has made to religion. And if we cannot find a framework ample enough to accommodate the facts or wide enough to cover them, then we say the facts have taken away our religion and we shall probably never recover it.

The inner history of every honest person is therefore a serious attempt to extend the boundaries of his religious thinking, and in particular his thought of God. I am reminded of one of the most revealing things ever said to me by another human being. I began my ministry under a wise and devout old man who preached to his people in a Massachusetts mill city an annual sermon on the latest discoveries in astronomy. One Monday morning I said to him, "I don't see the use of your annual sermon on astronomy to these people who are doing nothing but making and selling cotton cloth." He replied with fine contempt, "My dear boy, it's no use at all, but it greatly enlarges my idea of God." The history of religion has been in the past, and ought to be in the experience of every one of us, that of greatly enlarged ideas of God. For only by greatly enlarging our idea of God can we keep our religion through a lifetime, when so many facts are still out in the cold.

The trouble with much of our religion is that it is like the religion described in the first lesson for the morning (Isaiah 44:9-20). It is idolatrous. It is made up of the odds and ends of life which we have not been able to turn to any prior useful account, whittled into a crude image of ourselves, when, as the passage says with only too much truthfulness, we have nothing else to do.

Such is, indeed, the charge commonly and constantly brought against all religious ideas; they are anthropomorphic. We impute copies and caricatures of ourselves to the Infinite. This practice has always been so and is still so. Some of the great religious geniuses, the classical mystics in particular, refuse to make any statement whatsoever about God. God is the All, and to go beyond that statement is to limit God thereafter. God is the still darkness in which at last we lose ourselves. These ideas, however, are not intelligible or congenial to the practical Anglo-Saxon mind. If most of us are to think about God at all, we have to think by way of metaphors drawn from what we are and the life we know. We ought to realize, however, that when we speak of God as our Father we are using a figure of speech, not coining a scientific definition. Meanwhile, it is worth remembering that no little of our thinking in art and in science is being done in the same way. We do not profess that our pictures of things are visual photographs of reality; they are patterns of our own devising which seem to help us understand what is going on in the realm of truth and beauty.

I am saying these things because it ought to be increasingly clear to most of us that we need, religiously, greatly enlarged ideas of God. The teaching of Jesus himself hints at this fact constantly, though he seldom elaborated those hints. He left them to mature in the minds of his followers. The familiar parable of the good Samaritan is a case in point. The Jews had no dealings with the Samaritans. The good Samaritan was a contradiction in terms; there was no such person.

Take a recent instance. Some of us had the pleasure and honor of listening not long ago to Nehru. He is a devout Hindu. But he is also an educated, cosmopolitan, almost a sophisticated citizen of our twentieth century; a graduate of Harrow School and Cambridge University. As I listened to him I felt with fresh force that the missionary hymns of the last century were a bed that is too short for present-day facts and a covering too narrow for those facts. I could not feel of Nehru that he was a heathen in his blindness, bowing down to wood and stone. Nor could I feel that he was a soul benighted, denied the lamp of life unless I converted him to New England Congregationalism. In short, he made me realize with fresh force my need of greatly enlarged ideas of God.

I have been saying these things because they concern the possible contribution which religious-minded American Christians ought to be making to the cold facts of our modern world. There are no rules of thumb in the Bible to solve for us, in any mechanical way, the economic and political problems of our time. Christianity is concerned with premises and principles, rather than with rules. It is, above all else, a matter of one's initial attitude toward God and one's neighbor.

Unless I am mistaken, in a fallible memory, one of the great English Puritans of the seventeenth century said that when God wanted anything important done in this world he got an Englishman to do it. Given the gorgeous history of the Elizabethan age, that remark was not wholly unwarranted.

But we Americans of today are by no means immune to this presupposition.

In the middle of the seventeenth century New England experienced what was called the Great Awakening. That remarkable revival of religion led Jonathan Edwards to reason that God was probably about to conclude his work in history and usher in his final earthly kingdom. Edwards thought that it was only fair, since God had begun his work in the Old World, that he should make the New World the scene of its consummation. He said that Isaiah had prophesied that the final act would take place in the Isles of the Sea, but this could hardly mean England, because England was too near the Continent, and the Straits of Dover were not wide enough to fill the bill. He then concluded with a bit of local patriotism in which many of us can still recognize ourselves, "If we may suppose that this glorious work shall begin in any part of America, I think, if we consider the circumstances of the settlement of New England, it must needs appear the most likely of all the American colonies to be the place whence this work shall principally take its rise." Catholic Maryland, Quaker Pennsylvania, Anglican Virginia, Dutch Reformed New York are out in the cold.

To put it bluntly, there is great danger today that falling heir to the tempers, as well as the wealth and the prestige of Elizabethan and Puritan England, indeed the whole creditor status of England in the nineteenth century, we shall conclude that if God wants anything important done he will probably have to get an American to do it.

This subtle suggestion is shot through most of our thinking.

Acceptance of such a destiny is not necessarily unchristian. It depends on the way that this responsibility is accepted. Down one alley lies the temptation of the will-to-power, a very heady drink. Thus one of our distinguished military men said in Washington not long ago that if only the army, the navy and the air force would arrive at a unified policy we could lick the world. This may be so, but even so it is an imperfectly Christian account of our mission in history. Such are, however, the tempers which creep over us and into our minds and hearts. They are idolatries, as obvious as the idolatry which was described so vividly in our first lesson. And it is the business of Christianity to lay unremitting siege to all such suggestions. For such suggestions are too short a bed and too narrow a blanket to cover the facts.

Walter Bagehot once said that there is no pain in the world like the pain of a new idea. The painfulness of new ideas is felt more keenly in the area of religion than in any other area, simply because its ideas go so deep and involve so much. In sleepless impatience we may, if we will, get out of our too short beds and throw off our too narrow blankets and be done with religion, living hereafter without the steadying help of an idea of God that is large enough to cover the facts. We may, if we will, live naked in the world of cold facts.

The other alternative is to accept the fact that nothing is plainer in history than its awareness of constantly enlarging ideas of God. The Columbia anthropologist Boaz has said that the history of ethics is a matter of extending to the out-group moral standards which have been accepted for the in-group. The same is true of religion. Achieving such ideas for oneself is a costly business. It calls for modesty, humility, unselfishness, a forfeiting of much of the pride of life. It means stooping to conquer rather than overriding our world. Every one of us knows, in his own heart, where his idolatries and thus blind spots are. America today is in danger of becoming another Babylon and Assyria, another imperial Rome, another ruling Britannia, unless those of us who profess and call ourselves Christians can bring something of the mind of Christ to bear upon our national character. Christianity, witness Peter's vision in Acts 10, introduced into the world the pain of a greatly enlarged idea of God. You and I ought not to be strangers to that pain. Christianity is not a finished act of long ago; it is a process that is forever seeking to fulfill itself. Greatly enlarged ideas of God may not seem to be an immediately useful achievement; but one might defend the paradox that in the long run they turn out to be the most useful of all ideas.

> Lord God of Hosts, be with us yet,
>   Lest we forget—lest we forget!
>
> The tumult and the shouting dies;
>   The captains and the kings depart—
> Still stands Thine ancient Sacrifice,
>   An humble and a contrite heart.
> Lord God of Hosts, be with us yet,
>   Lest we forget—lest we forget!
>
> * * * *
>
> For frantic boast and foolish word,
>   Thy mercy on Thy people, Lord!
> Amen.[1]

---

[1] Rudyard Kipling, "Recessional," from *The Five Nations.* Copyright, 1903, 1931, by Rudyard Kipling. Used by permission of Mrs. George Bambridge, Doubleday & Company, Inc., and A. P. Watt & Son.

V

THE VIRTUE OF COMPASSION

Text: I also could speak as ye do: if your soul were in my soul's stead.—JOB 16:4

THE book of Job is in the main a conversation among Job and three friends known as Eliphaz the Temanite, Bildad the Shuhite, and Zophar the Naamathite.

The contrast between these proper names is striking. Job was "a man in the land of Uz." These clipped monosyllables fit the man himself; he was a person who had been trained down, disciplined by life. Whereas his polysyllabic friends from polysyllabic places had not undergone any such training and self-discipline.

Job was in trouble, real trouble, and his friends were professedly trying to help him. He had had pains of the body, but these were not his worst pain. His worst pain was that in his mind. He reminds us of King Lear out on the blasted heath in the storm, "The tempest in my mind doth make all else seem calm."

The conversation among the four of them goes on for thirty chapters, but it never gets anywhere nor proves anything. Job had been hurt; he was puzzled and angry, angry with life, angry with his fellow men, angry with God. His main difficulty was that he could not understand what had happened to him, and why it happened to him in particular. For the moment he made these three men the butt of his anger—"miserable comforters" he called them. He was never polite to them nor patient with them nor even fair to them. It says a good deal for their self-restraint that they kept on listening to him so long.

On the other hand it must be admitted that they were rather irritating. They were saying the correct thing in a complacent and orthodox way. They were not pharisaical or insincere, but they were thoroughly conventional. The difficulty would seem to have been this: they were trying to help a man in trouble, when they had never had any trouble themselves.

This whole long first part of the book of Job is like a certain type of conversation in which we have often found ourselves involved. It is not that we are talking at cross-purposes with someone else, but rather that we are talking to *no* purpose. Our minds never really meet, because we have no common ground of experience on which to stand, nor premises on which we are agreed.

Thus, in the words of the text, Job put his finger on what is the real difficulty in such a situation, "I also could speak as ye do: if your soul were in my soul's stead." In other words, "If you could put yourself in my place and I could put myself in your place, we might understand each other and help each other."

Here and there in the Old Testament we have prophecies of the coming of the Messiah. The greatest of these prophecies are not so much predictions of a specific event in future time as foreshadowings, hints of what was to be the character of Christ. In this sense of the word we might say that our text from Job is a bit of Messianic prophecy. There have been many theories as to the nature of the divinity of Christ, but they all start from a single inference drawn from the life of Jesus; he put himself in our place, and in turn asks us to put ourselves in his place. He "was made in the likeness of men," says St. Paul, "and being found in fashion as a man." "In all things," says the writer to the Hebrews, "it behoved him to be made like unto his brethren." Whenever the unlikeness of Jesus to us has been so overemphasized that it has impaired this strong initial sense of his identification with us, the result is what the church has always called a heresy.

We are living at a time when it is very difficult to see just what the Christian religion may fairly be expected to contribute to our troubled world. But might we say that a Christian ought to be a person who can put himself in the other man's place. This does not mean, necessarily, that he will approve of all that the other man thinks and says and does, but it does mean that he will understand how the other man came to be as he is; as we say in the vernacular, "how he got that way."

There are a vast number of people in the world who seem anxious to do good to others, but who will do good only on their own terms. We meet them on committees, we watch them manage our philanthropies, we find them at work in politics, national and international. They are not bad, but somehow they are imperfectly Christian. They are, if the truth be told in Job's words, "miserable comforters" of our humanity, because they stand aloof from it; they have never identified themselves with it.

Their difficulty may be this: that all their lives they have been able to content themselves with a kind of secondhand life. The platitudes they have inherited from the past have sufficed them. Perhaps they are fortunate. Yet one can only feel that somehow they have missed what being alive at all can mean and ought to mean.

With most of us the difficulty is of another kind. For we suffer today, not from a dearth of experience, but from a surfeit of experience. Mankind, as a whole, has never before had to live through as much as has been the lot of our generation. This surfeit of experience was beginning to be felt even before World War I. Forty years ago Father George Tyrrell said, "It seems to me that our experience is given us to be the food of our character and spiritual life; but, in point of fact, we spend our whole life storing up food and never have leisure to lie down quietly, with the cows in the field, and ruminate, bit by bit, what we have swallowed so hastily." Of all forms of waste, the waste of experience is the most tragic.

Critics of classical drama have often pointed out that the essence of tragedy is not the conflict of good and evil, that is relatively simple. Nor is it suffering and misfortune, painful as these may be. The essence of tragedy is always the presence of what seems to be some needless waste, waste of ideals, waste of affections, waste of sorrow and sacrifice, waste of life itself.

In this sense of the word our time has been, and may yet go on being, a terribly tragic time. The waste of the experience of the years from 1914 to 1945 has been vast and terrifying. No immediate personal problem which, one by one, we now face is more grave than this. Is that waste to go on? We are gorged with experiences which we have not yet digested; we have become so habituated to excitement that like the old Romans at their feasts we are half inclined to go out and make ourselves sick in order to come back for more excitement. But that would be a sheer and tragic waste of life, if it be true that experience is given us, not for the sake of the sensation we get from it, but rather that it may be the food of our character and spiritual life. To have learned nothing from these years through which we have been living will be to have lived a merely wasted life. If this be true of those of us who have lived in safety and great comfort here at home, how doubly true it will be of those of us back from the wars whose experiences have been stern and hard in far-off lands.

Hear what a student had to say on coming to the University after being in World War II: "During my three years' duty aboard an aircraft carrier as communications officer, I saw many men floundering in disordered lives which lacked a central integration: I saw them seek that integration in almost every conceivable form. It was plain to see that only those men with spiritual backbone were the ones who withstood not only the rigors of combat duty, but also—and this was infinitely more difficult—the rigors of moral combat duty which one constantly undergoes in the service. These years in the navy were a profound experience—spiritually, mentally, morally—and it is my sincere desire to use wisely the lessons learned during them." This man's experience may have been hard—it probably was hard—but there is no tragedy in it. The years that are just ended for him will not be wasted by him.

What he says leads us on to the heart of the matter. Our experience of life may be in the first instance the stuff of personal private character. But it is something more than that. It is a passkey into the lives of others. There are three words which describe what ought to be our more generous attitudes toward vast areas of humanity today: the first is pity, the second is compassion, the third is sympathy. There is a difference between the first of these words and the other two. Gilbert Murray in one of his prefaces to the Greek tragedies tells us what the difference is. Pity, he says, is an aristocratic virtue; compassion and sympathy are democratic virtues. Pity condescends; compassion and sympathy share. The last two words come, one from the Latin and the other from the Greek, but they both mean the same thing; they mean sharing the experiences of others.

The English novelist, Mark Rutherford, once said, "In the worst of maladies . . . the healing effect which is produced by the visit of a friend who can simply say, 'I have endured all that,' is most marked."

We have in those words the secret of the appeal of Jesus to our minds and hearts. He was tempted just as we are. He was hungry and homeless as millions are today. He was misunderstood and rejected and lonely. The greatest thing we know about pain, says a New Testament scholar, is that Jesus felt it. And for the Christian the significance of these facts rests on the conviction that God himself is not content with a divine and aristocratic pity for his children; but that he has compassion on them and sympathizes with them.

We have here a clue as to the Christian use of whatever experiences we may have had over these last years. Some of these experiences were for many of us very hard; others suffered much less. But life has not been easy for any of us. Yet we are here alive, in security and as the world goes in great comfort. Our happy circumstance might prompt us to be content with pitying the rest of the world. But that temper will never get us or the world very far. For there is in our humanity some proper pride, some native dignity, some deep-rooted self-respect which prompts the comeback, "I don't want your pity. I prefer to do without it."

Therefore, we are challenged to fall back on such of our harder experiences as can be translated into the stuff of sympathy and compassion. Your real problem as a Christian is, therefore, this: How far can you honestly put yourself in the place of another whom you would really like to help? How far can you say, "I have endured all that," or if you have not endured it to the full, "I have at least endured enough to understand something of your life and your lot, even though it be from far off"? One can safely assert that from the Christian standpoint the hurts of our time will never be healed by an aristocratic pity. They require the democratic and Christian virtue of sympathy.

There remains, however, one final problem. You may not pretend to experiences you have not had, and all of us know quite well that there are ills in the world that lie beyond our experience. The permutations and combinations of happenings to human beings are infinite in number. No two lives coincide, and, given the totality of man's experience, what any one of us may know and feel is very little. How then are we to match a limited life to the limitless occasion for sympathy.

Georges Duhamel, who began his life as a surgeon in the French Army over thirty years ago, says in the first of his books written in a military hospital that wars go on because there is no way at all by which one man can feel in his own body the pain which another man suffers. For if each man and all men could feel that pain, there would never be another war.

The best we can do is try to cultivate patiently that unselfishness of mind and heart which we know as imagination. When human relationships break down, that breakdown, whatever else may be involved, always implies a failure on someone's part to put himself in the place of another. This is the weak link, ending often as a broken link, in homes, in churches, in races, in states. The white Gentile is inclined to talk in a condescending way about the Negro problem and the Jewish problem. But he has never tried to feel what it is like to be relegated to a Jim Crow car in the South, or turned away from an apartment house in the North. It is not the Negro or the Jew who is his initial problem. His first problem is his own unimaginative self. He will never contribute much to the solution of those other problems until he has solved that prior and more intimate problem. He will be, in Job's words, a "miserable comforter" of mankind until he has cultivated the power to put his soul in their soul's stead.

Remember the end of Shaw's play *Saint Joan?* The Maid has been burned at the stake in Rouen. Years afterward some of the characters concerned meet again. A bumbling participant in the original action, the Chaplain de Stogumber, is saying that he has been saved. Saved, says the Bishop of Beauvais, by the sufferings of Christ. Not at all, says de Stogumber—saved by the sight of a very cruel happening he once saw. One must have seen it to understand it. It was terrible. But it saved him, though he had been a little astray in his wits ever since. And then the Bishop asks a question which goes very deep and far, "Must then a Christ perish in torment in every age to save those who have no imagination?"

VI

RELIGION AS A SENSE OF PROPORTION

Text: Yet show I unto you a more excellent way.—

I Corinthians 12:31

SOMEONE has said that finding the meaning of a word is like trying to persuade a gull to light on the stern of a ship. In so doing, one must not shoot the gull and tie it to the rigging. It must be alive when it lights.

This is doubly true in the case of the elemental words in the language. One can move around these words and see them from different angles, but the view of the word from any one angle is an aspect of it, not the whole truth of it. Mount Monadnock, in southern New Hampshire seen from Jaffrey is one thing, but seen from Dublin it is quite another thing.

This is particularly true of the great words in the Bible. They can be illustrated; they were never defined in some neat verbal packet. Thus Jesus never defined his one central idea, the Kingdom of God; rather he said, seen from here it looks this way, seen from there it looks that way. Bible scholars tell us that this was and is the habit of the Hebrew mind.

The thirteenth chapter of I Corinthians ends with three of the greatest words in the Bible, in religion, indeed in our whole vocabulary: faith and hope and charity. The first of these words has at least four or five distinct meanings in the New Testament. In the teaching of Jesus it means trust in God; in the writings of Paul it means personal devotion to Christ; in the Epistle to the Hebrews it means creative endeavor; in the pastoral epistles it means loyalty to tradition. All these meanings are important. So with the word "hope"; in the more skeptical part of the Bible it suggests the odd chance that things may turn out better tomorrow than they are today. In the more confident parts of the Bible it is the conviction that since God and the world are what they are things must be better and will be better.

The most elusive of these three words is the last and, as St. Paul intimates, the greatest. The King James version translated that word as "charity." This translation is now probably inaccurate and inadequate since we think of charity as a matter of our philanthropies. But it is a fair question how faithful to Paul's meaning the word "love" is, which is used in all modern translations. Today most persons associate that word with the passion of man for woman and woman for man. There was a word for that passion available at Paul's hand, but he did not use it. Indeed that word, "eros," simply does not appear in the New Testament. What is called erotic symbolism eventually began to appear in Christian writings. It was never carried as far in Christianity as it has been in many other religions. And today it is felt to be fraught with many emotional and psychological dangers. In any case the word which might warrant any trace of eroticism in the idea of love is simply absent from the New Testament, save for the occasional chaste reference to the Church as the bride of Christ.

There are two other words which are used in the New Testament. One implies what might be called warm-hearted affection. It is the word which gives us the first half of the name of Philadelphia, the city of brotherly love.

And then there is another word which Paul uses in his thirteenth chapter of I Corinthians, the elusive word "agape." This word means more than warm-hearted friendship. Yet it stands quite clear of the emotional involvements in the word for sexual love. It is a rather cool word. The best account of it I know says that whatever else the word may imply, it implies a "steady set of the will." This will is directed to the good of its object. The idea of loving God is for many persons a meaningless one. We hardly know how to set about it. In the Old Testament the idea of loving God is identified with obeying his laws and keeping his commandments. So when we pray that God's Kingdom may come and his will be done our prayer is an act of love; our will is steadily set upon God's good. As for our human relations the word has little or nothing to do with our likes and dislikes, which we cannot control. In any case, liking your neighbor, as Jesus said, is a matter of temperament or circumstance, and has no moral or religious merit. Loving your enemy may seem to be impossible, since it is a contradiction in terms. But religiously you can love your enemy, even though you may not like him, since even as his enemy you are still under bonds to seek his good. Now I have no intention to try to shoot down this word and tie its dead body to the rigging. What I have in mind, rather, is to say something about the whole marvelous chapter in I Corinthians, which it climaxes and crowns.

St. Paul's First Epistle to the Corinthians may not be the most important book in the New Testament, but it is one of the most interesting. We usually think of the chapter on love as being a beautiful bit of poetry to be lifted out of its setting of dull prose. The more one reads the epistle as a whole, the clearer it is that this view of the chapter is entirely false. I Corinthians 13 is the keystone of an arch. Let us grant its poetry. But an equally good case can be made for the theory that it is one of the soberest bits of cold, hard prose that was ever written.

The epistle as a whole is an answer to a series of questions which the Church at Corinth had referred to Paul for his answers. They may have written these questions to him; they may have relayed them by personal messenger. Some of the questions are theological; still more of them are ethical or moral. Taken seriatim as they appear in the epistle they concern first divisions in the Church, what we should call denominational differences and sectarian rivalries. Another problem concerns a difficult case of sexual perversion. Then there is the question of Paul's right to be called an apostle and of what might be called the validity of private conscience. There is next a long discussion of the social manners of a Christian who is at every point involved in a non-Christian society. The problem of marriage or celibacy is debated. Then we come to the jealousies among members of an already complicated church community. It does not take very much imagination to translate most of these problems into their modern equivalents. It is this modernity of a very ancient book which gives it, for most of us, its contemporaneity.

It is interesting to see how honest Paul is in face of the difficult situations which had been put up to him. He does not pretend to be infallible or even authoritative. He says that at some points he thinks he has the word of the Lord; but again at other points he makes no such claim and says that his answers are his own opinion, his best opinion, but he cannot guarantee them as being right. Once more this modesty, this tentativeness, is very modern and, we might add, very Protestant.

Now one can imagine Paul's being confronted by this congested collection of hard problems and saying to himself, "This communication from Corinth is going to be hard to answer," and then laying it aside for a while to mull over it. There comes, however, a day when he sits down and tackles what is his present epistle, working along through one question after another. Finally he comes to a point when he seems to say to himself, "There is great danger that I and my parishioners in Corinth may lose sight of the wood because of the trees. With the best will in the world we are getting involved in too many details. We may conclude that the answer to one of these questions, or the sum of all the answers, is Christianity, and that is not so. We must somehow recover our imperiled sense of perspective. We must try by a deliberate act of recollection to make up our minds what matters more, what matters most, in religion." Having come to this conclusion he then says, "All these ways we have been discussing may be good, each in its own way, but I show you a better way." Having so said, he launches into the thirteenth chapter, which we know so well.

Coming up to the chapter in this way we can understand the quality of hard prose which runs through it. The total chapter is and must always be felt to be poetic. But it is poetry of a nonsentimental kind. The chapter often seems to me to have an almost scientific brevity and clarity. In his attempt to decide what matters most in Christianity Paul is ruthless in discarding a great many of the assets of our religion simply on the ground that, important as they are, they are not all-important. Faith in its dogmatic forms, prophecy which means great preaching, philanthropy carried to the point of self-impoverishment, the martyrdom of the body, and even knowledge itself—all these change and vanish away. They do not last, they have no staying power. We grow up, our opinions and convictions change, we outgrow our immaturity. But what lasts is the three tempers of mind and heart, the three constant attitudes toward God and man and the world, and the greatest of these is love, the steady set of the will toward the good of that which we love.

Paul was facing a situation which is by no means as yet resolved. His letter to the Corinthians and this chapter in particular are of perennial interest because they represent one of the first deliberate attempts in Christian history to gear the absolute and uncompromising idealism of the life and teaching of Christ to our very unideal world.

And if in perplexity and often discouragement we say that the two cannot ever be made to mesh, we may take heart from Paul's good courage as we find it in I Corinthians. In one of his last books Professor Whitehead says, "The progress of humanity can be defined as the process of transforming society so as to make the original Christian ideals increasingly practicable for its individual members. As society is now constituted a literal adherence to the moral precepts scattered through the Gospels would mean sudden death"; nevertheless, "these Christian ideals remain a gauge by which to test the defects of human society. So long as the Galilean images are but the dreams of an unrealized world, so long must they spread the infection of an uneasy spirit."

Religion is often relegated to the realm of poetry alone. That is a mistake. After his first furlough in Europe following his earliest years in Africa, Albert Schweitzer went back to his little hospital in Lambaréné. He says of this return that all the poetry of his original venture had gone and the prose of Africa was hard upon him. Fortunately, he knew enough about religion and was a good enough Christian to understand what would be implied in writing his own thirteenth chapter of I Corinthians.

We are living at a time when the poetry of religion, indeed the poetry of much of life itself, is not felt as deeply as once it may have been. Ours is, for the present at least, one of the prose ages of history. But no one can ever know whether the poetry of life is true until he has proved it in life's prose. Each one of us has to challenge and criticize and jettison a good deal of what may have seemed to him the necessary apparatus of his religion, which after all often vanishes on its own account, to review his own experience and discover what has mattered most and what has lasted through the years. He ought to relive the First Epistle of the Corinthians, and if he has caught something of the genius of Christianity he ought to know, even in his prosiest hours, that love beareth all . things, endureth all things and never faileth.

VII

THE LORD'S PRAYER—I

Text: And it came to pass, that, as he was praying in a certain place, when he ceased, one of his disciples said unto him, Lord, teach us to pray.—LUKE 11:1

THE Lord's Prayer was the answer to this request. That prayer is today perhaps the one best bond of union between all sorts and conditions of Christians. However they may differ in their creeds, they can always say this prayer together. If all of us argued less and prayed more this would be a more Christian world than it now is.

Jesus never intended the prayer that bears his name to become a fixed item in a liturgy. His own church—the Jewish synagogue—was not a formally liturgical church, and he himself was an informal person. Our Puritan forefathers seldom or never used the Lord's Prayer in their church services. Their distaste for constant use of the prayer was part of their thoroughgoing revolt from the Roman Mass and even the Anglican Prayer Book. It is hard for us today to recover the mind of a generation for which the Lord's Prayer was taboo because it was printed in a book. We are better off with it— much better off—than our too fussy forefathers were without it. Of all the acts in Christian worship, it is today the most universal and for that reason the most precious.

On the other hand, we must not forget that as first pronounced by Jesus, it was not a finished form for some new Christian liturgy. It was, rather, a suggestive guide to prayer, a framework which we might fill out and elaborate as we chose—nevertheless, a basic pattern to which all prayer should in principle conform. If our prayers depart radically from this pattern, there is, from the standpoint of the Gospels, something wrong with them. They need correction by "the mind of Christ" as intimated in the Lord's Prayer.

The prayer occurs twice in the Gospels, once in the Sermon on the Mount in the Gospel of Matthew, and once, quite independently, in the Gospel of Luke. I should think it more probable that St. Luke's account of the origin of the prayer is right. It was not, as in St. Matthew, a brief paragraph in a long sermon concerned with many other matters as well. In St. Luke's account the story explains itself. The disciples, sensing that Jesus knew more about prayer than they knew, and that they needed to know something of what he knew, asked him to teach them how to pray. This all seems probable and natural and right.

It is significant that they should have come awake to the fact that they could be taught how to pray and needed to be taught. Even to this day most of us would admit that we need to be, and can be, taught many other things; but that we need to be taught how to pray is an idea which comes to us later in our religious life rather than earlier, and comes as something of a discovery. Prayer, to most of us, is a matter of asking for what we want at the moment, and letting it go at that. Dr. Fosdick, in one of the best-known modern definitions of prayer, says that prayer is "dominant desire." Prayer is certainly not a matter of occasional or incidental desire; it is a dominant mood. But we cannot assume, and Dr. Fosdick does not for a moment assume, that our desires, however dominant they may be at any given moment, deserve gratification. The mere fact that I want something very much, that I tell God so, and ask him to give it to me, is no assurance that I ought to have it. Or that I will get it. Our impulsive habits of prayer need to be corrected by Huxley's remark, "I have observed that the universe is not very much affected by my likes and dislikes." It was just such a sober second thought that prompted long ago and ought still to prompt the request, "Lord, teach us to pray."

With these thoughts in mind I have had in mind for some time taking two Sunday mornings to meditate on the Lord's Prayer. If we were to hear the prayer for the first time we should surely be struck by its swift brevity and its concreteness. Part of the danger of knowing it so well and saying it so habitually is the risk we run of not thinking about it as we say it. Its words become bits of paper hung on a prayer wheel that spins aimlessly in the winds. Yet I know little in the Bible that bears thinking about quite as well.

A writer of a generation ago, Mark Rutherford, said, in blunt terms, that "the mind and heart of the average church-

goer need to be shifted from what is *self* to what is *not* self."
To effect that shift is a matter of self-discipline, something one
has to learn to do. It is a matter of getting God, and all that
God stands for, in the place that is too often and too naturally
occupied by one's self.

Well, that is what strikes us about the Lord's Prayer the
moment we begin to think about it. In the order of its petitions, God's things are put first: his name, his kingdom, his
will. It is only ofter we have prayed for these things that we
may then go on to pray for the things that are secondary, our
own things.

What, then, are the valid things which we may properly
ask for ourselves? What self-centered petitions have the
approval of Christ?

It is important to notice that there are such things. Some
types of religion—the more extreme of which are called
mysticism—tell us that we ought not to ask anything at all for
ourselves; that self is the seat and root of sin, and ought to be
wholly denied. It is worth pointing out that these attempts to
get wholly rid of self do not have the sanction of the Lord's
Prayer. As in the statement that we are to love our neighbors
as ourselves, so in the prayer we may in all earnestness say,
"Give us, forgive us, lead us, deliver us." The Lord's Prayer
does not encourage what might be called psychologically futile
attempts to pretend that we have no selves.

The first petition which we make in our own behalf is,
"Give us this day our daily bread." This is a prayer in behalf
of whatever is necessary, and all that is necessary, for the
decent maintenance of the life of the body. Bread means not

bread as against meat, but food in general. It means, by inference, needful shelter and clothing. It is the answer to all that is implied by being hungry and thirsty, naked and homeless. There is, then, no sanction for the theory, held by so many religions, that matter is evil and the body itself sinful. To this extent the Lord's Prayer states the case for what has been called the religion of healthy-mindedness, as against unnatural asceticism. Such, indeed, is the whole impression one gets from the person and the life of Jesus.

Dean Luther A. Weigle has said that the word "daily" so translated occurs only twice in the Bible, and nowhere else in the Greek language. It has been said that the word may mean "today's bread"—on the theory that tomorrow will take care of itself. In that case the word would have the old story of manna in the desert, given fresh each day, as a background. Or it may mean bread "day by day."

But the more probable meaning is, Give us the bread that is needful for us, what we must have to support life. One could go on from this premise to develop the whole theory of the medieval Church as to the institution of property. We are to be allowed to have and to own what we can actually use for living; we may not go on to accumulate more than that as a means of power over others. What is meant by "bread" in particular is, by inference, to be true of the rest of the necessities of life. We may properly ask God for them. Many religions other than Christianity, and a good many persons within Christianity, hold that religious insights may be had by morbid and unnatural attacks upon the body. There is nothing of this idea in the teaching of Jesus or in this prayer. We may leave this petition with some wise words which Rufus Jones wrote not long ago, "In so far as unhealthy traits have persisted they have been a liability and a handicap. It has been over the highway of health rather than over the bridge of disease that the largest freight of truth has come to us."

"Forgive us our trespasses, as we forgive those who trespass against us." As a matter of faithfulness to the original the words in the Matthew version are probably more accurate, "Forgive us our *debts,* as we forgive our *debtors.*" It may be mainly sins that are to be forgiven, but it is more than sin. Jesus more than once talked in his parables about the man who was in debt. Sometimes his debtor's lot may have been because of his own wrongdoing; at other times it was a matter of his whole place in society.

It is said that very few people today have any sense of sin. Perhaps not, in the old-fashioned meaning of the word. And yet I wonder. Some deep sense of moral uneasiness is very hard to get rid of. It has always seemed to me that Arthur Hugh Clough stated what is an all but universal experience when he said:

> Like a child
> In some strange garden left alone,
> I pace about the pathways of the world,
> Plucking light hopes and joys from every stem,
> With qualms of vague misgiving in my heart,
> That payment at the last will be required,
> Payment I cannot make.

Thirty years ago a minor English poet, F. W. Bourdillon,

put this idea in other words which have become even more true today than they were then, when he wrote:

> In earth or heaven,
> > Bold sailor on the sea,
> What have I given
> That you should die for me.

> What can I give,
> > O soldier leal and brave,
> Long as I live,
> To pay the life you gave.

The idea of our "debts" may at times be sharpened down to our actual wrongdoing, but at other times they are no less than the wide-ranging thought of these lines.

There are things one cannot ever pay for in this life. They can only be taken humbly with thanks. The debt which they represent can only be forgiven. That is all that can be done about it.

Meanwhile, consider how very prominent the idea of forgiveness, and the word itself, are in the teaching of Jesus. His most famous and probably his most familiar parable is that of the prodigal son. It is above all else a story of a father's forgiveness. We are often told that the idea of "love" is the one that was uppermost in the mind of Jesus. But, if we look over the first three Gospels, in which we get most faithfully his accent and the echo of his voice, the word "love" is almost never found. The word which does duty for it is this other word "forgiveness." And forgiveness, so far from being a temper and act alien to love, would seem to be love about its most difficult task, love standing the severest test. Jesus lays siege to our hard hearts, for every one of us is hardhearted at some point, and he asks, "Can you and will you forgive?" Then he always adds, not so much as an argument or an incentive, but as an afterthought, "If not, how can you expect others to forgive you?" There is no one-way traffic for forgiveness. There is no Dead Sea into which forgiveness flows for us, but from which there is no outlet into the lives of others.

"Lead us not into temptation." Of all the petitions of the Lord's Prayer this is the most unintelligible. The idea that God tempts us would seem to be wrong at the outset. Even if he does allow a world in which we are tempted because we are free, we do not think of him as, then, leading us himself into temptation. Indeed, in another place the Bible goes out of its way to deny this idea. The Epistle of James says, "Let no man say when he is tempted, I am tempted of God: for God cannot be tempted with evil, neither tempteth he any man." There is another passage which stands halfway between the Lord's Prayer and this verse from St. James. It seems to agree that God allows a world in which we can be tempted, and therefore is to that extent responsible for our temptation, but that in this case he will come to our help. Thus St. Paul says, "There hath no temptation taken you but such as is common to man: but God is faithful, who will not suffer you to be tempted above that ye are able; but will with the temptation also make a way to escape." This is the common interpretation of the petition in the Lord's Prayer. God does put us to the proof, but we may hope that he will not prove us too much.

There is, however, a quite different interpretation which I venture to suggest. Personally, I think it is probably the right one. The word translated "temptation" had in New Testament times a technical, as well as a general, meaning. It was the name given to what was supposed to be the final struggle of good and evil in history, the great, last Armageddon. It would be terrible beyond all imagining, but after it was over the Kingdom would come. This trial would be, perhaps, more than man ought to be asked to bear. If this be what the prayer means then its mood is precisely that of Jesus' prayer in the garden of Gethsemane, "Father, if it be possible, let this cup pass from me." If you were to seek what might be a contemporary and perhaps secular restatement of this petition in the Lord's Prayer it might well be, "Save us from the Third World War."

And finally, "Deliver us from evil." This may mean evil in the abstract, evil in general. It more probably means, "the Evil One"—the Devil himself.

Most people do not believe in the Devil today, and therefore do not need to ask to be delivered from him. I venture one comment. Our attitude toward evil is not what it was a generation ago. Then it was, for most of us, an imperfection, something that was in process of being outgrown and sloughed off. Today evil has been incarnated in human beings to a degree that we should never have thought possible.

You do not modernize the Lord's Prayer out of all relation to the original if you say, "Deliver me from the devilishness of mankind, deliver me from the devil in man." In fact, nothing else in the Lord's Prayer is as easy to understand today, or needs more to be said.

And thus, "Thine is the kingdom and the power and the glory, forever and ever. Amen."

VIII

THE LORD'S PRAYER—2

Text: I bow my knees unto the Father of our Lord Jesus Christ.
Of whom the whole family in heaven and earth is named.—
EPHESIANS 3:14, 15

EARLIER we considered the last half of the Lord's Prayer
which contains the petitions we make in our own behalf.
This morning, I am reverting to the first half of the Lord's
Prayer in which we are bidden to pray for God's name and
God's Kingdom and God's will. Most of us, until we have
trained ourselves in this matter, pray, first for ourselves, then
for others, and finally for God's concerns. The Lord's Prayer,
on the contrary, starts with the things that are God's and
after that goes on to the things that are ours.

The prayer begins, *"Our* Father." The plural possessive
pronoun reveals one of the characteristics of the Christian
religion. Another great system in the ancient world describes
religion in the splendid phrase, "The flight of the alone to the
Alone," that is, of the single solitary man to the solitary God.

The Christian religion is not without its strain of loneliness, but this loneliness is not its full or final temper. It has been said that for most other religions God and one man suffice, but that the Christian religion calls for God and two men.

"Our *Father.*" The last word is, probably, the one word most characteristic of our religion. Whatever else Christians have believed or disbelieved, they have agreed to call God their Father. If this word is, historically, the most characteristic of all Christian words, it is at the same time the boldest word that any religion can say. To many persons in our time it presents such difficulties that they can hardly say it at all, with good conscience. It is as though, in our day, this classic Christian name for God were lapsing back into most ancient times, when with the Jews of long ago the name of God was so mysterious that it was never spoken.

Thus, Thomas Huxley wrote to Charles Kingsley, "I cannot see one shadow or tittle of evidence that the great unknown underlying the phenomena of the universe stands to us in the relation of a Father." The number of intelligent and serious-minded persons who share Huxley's position has greatly increased since his day.

This is not the moment to discuss the arguments for belief in the existence of God. We can walk over that familiar and difficult ground some other day. We are for the moment concerned with the relevance of the word "Father" to the nature of a God in whom we already believe.

Remember, in the first place, that the word is not and cannot be a definition. It is a metaphor, a figure of speech. It is what one of the great preachers to this University of a generation ago, Dr. George A. Gordon, used to call an "Aspect of the Infinite Mystery."

Therefore, it is hardly fair of the critics of Christianity to say, as a correspondent in a recent number of the *Harvard Alumni Bulletin* says, that he can no longer believe in a divine facsimile of some earthly bewhiskered old gentleman. If we are going to think about God at all, we have one of two options: we must think about him in the terms of human life at its best, or we must decide that it is impossible to think about him at all. A religion must either make use of our human experience, as providing an analogy for its own thought, or it must be content to label God as the "transcendent X" and let it go at that.

If we concede that we must find our most suggestive and valid metaphors for religious thinking in our own human life, then we may go on to say that, of all human relationships, that of fatherhood is, on the whole, the best. The one other metaphor which religions have often used is that of the man and the woman, the lover and the beloved. However, this metaphor has too often proved emotionally and even morally dangerous. It lacks the coolness and the serenity of the idea of fatherhood. Fifty years ago my own father gave me a book of Phillips Brooks' which said, "In all its human uses, the idea of fatherhood comes nearer to being a religious idea than that of any other human relationship." I have never seen any reason to question that statement.

But there is one thing we need to remember. In the elder world, in which Jesus lived, a Father was the center of human values; life was organized about him. Men have their reasonable needs which are entitled to be met. Jesus takes them for granted. "Your heavenly Father knoweth that ye have need of all these things." Therefore, as against far too many modern homes, the emphasis on the idea of the fatherhood in the mind of Christ is not so much what a father owes a son as what a son owes a father. For the mind of Christ, we are God's children, we are here to do his work, and not to please ourselves. The moral reference is from ourselves to God, not from God to us.

"Who art in heaven." Once again, it is as easy to smile at the pearly gates of heaven as at the long-whiskered God of the theological cartoonist. And it is quite true that Copernicus ruined the biblical idea of heaven as a place up in the sky. The case has been magnificently stated by George Tyrrell in these words,

> If our astronomy has in some way enlarged, it has also impoverished, our notion of the heavens. It has given us quantitative mysteries in exchange for qualitative. As the mind travels endlessly into space it meets only with more orbs and systems of orbs in their millions, an infinite monotony of matter and motion. But never does it strike against some boundary wall of the universe beyond which God keeps an eternal Sabbath in a new order of existence. The heaven that lay behind the blue curtain of the sky whence by night God hung out his silver lamps to shine upon the earth, was a far deeper symbol of the eternal home than the cold and shelterless deserts of astronomical space.

For religion the truth, and thus the importance, of this moving passage lies in the statement that we have exchanged a qualitative mystery for a quantitative mystery. Even in the New Testament the core of its thought of heaven is not so much faith in another place than this world, as faith in a different kind of world. In heaven there are no liars or sorcerers or idolaters or whoremongers; there is no more death, there is no sorrow or crying or pain. In heaven God shall wipe away all tears from their eyes.

And all this, for religion, is not a social ideal to be realized at some remote time in human history; it is an account of a realm of things that already exists and is real. This is a Christian idea, but it is not merely a Christian idea. It had been the Jewish idea; it was the heart of Plato's whole doctrine of ideas. If one doubts the general truth of the Christian idea of heaven, one dismisses at the same time Judaism and Platonism. Looking back over the last thirty or forty years one finds it hard to say that we have been living in a real world. We have lived in a world acutely, tragically, poignantly actual. But it strains one's credulity to call it real in the religious sense. Indeed it must often seem to us hideously unreal. "Who art in heaven" is, even at this late date, as it was at the first, a profession of faith in a realm of things more real than that which we know here and now, and made more real to our imagination, by its contrast to the "smoke and stir of this dim spot which men call Earth." Remember, then, that heaven is not a place of living but a kind and quality of life.

"Hallowed be thy name." In this sentence we are living in a world where a man's name is an index of his concerns and his character. The term "name" in the Bible is not merely a tag or a number plate for identification in a census or an army file. It is a transcript of what the man is in himself. We are back in the early Anglo-Saxon days when the name carried all these connotations: Mr. Baker, Mr. Farmer, Mr. Fisher, Mr. Clark, Mr. Parson, and the like.

The hallowing of the name of God is, therefore, something more than the matter of avoiding a merely verbal profanity. Most people who swear do not stop to think what they are saying; it is a mere matter of habit. But it is worth remembering what Chesterton once said, that if we find a word being used in profanity, we may be certain that it has to do with elemental things. Men do not use trivial terms in their profanity.

Therefore the Lord's Prayer is, at this point, concerned with all that is meant by the character of God: his eternity, his holiness, his wisdom, his love, his forgiveness. The prayer asks that we shall hold all manifestations of these characteristics and attributes as sacred. If we are religious persons we will never make fun of any of these traits of the divine as they are revealed by persons around us, or as we impute them to God. When we come into their presence we will know that we are on holy ground.

Our personal appraisals of the idea of the sacred vary. What is sacred to me may not be sacred to you. Let that go. The point is, is there some area which for you is sacred, and which you would never consciously profane? You would never make a joke about it, or treat it lightly; you would treasure it, and if need be fight for it, and even die for it. For the perfectly irreligious man is the man who has left in his life no feeling for anything that is sacred. Coleridge once said that philosophy begins in wonder and ends in wonder, and that the interspace is filled with admiration. With the change of a single word the same thing may be said of religion: Religion begins in wonder and ends in wonder, and the interspace is filled with reverence.

"Thy Kingdom come." Once again a metaphor from a political world with which we broke a century and a half ago. The whole idea of Kingship is getting to be ancient history. How many times have you shared lately in the perennial discussion as to the validity and the usefulness of the British crown? Theologically we sloughed off what has been called the "Sultanic" idea of God, the God of Calvin and Edwards, two hundred years ago.

In the New Testament, however, the word "Kingdom" is not dependent upon the idea of absolute monarchy. The term means, primarily, "realm"; i.e., an organized area under a single jurisdiction. I think one can get some idea of what that old phrase "the Kingdom of God" means by considering for a moment the aura of the antithetical term "world" in the New Testament. It is a strange word, with something about it both alluring and repellent. It is a word that one is both drawn toward and yet afraid of. It was, I think, Bishop Gore who fashioned the very penetrating saying that the term "world" in the New Testament is intended to describe the social life of man organized apart from God. The truth of worldliness is, therefore, secularity. We cannot deny the vast amount of worldliness in the life of our time. As that British chaplain, Neville Talbot, put it thirty years ago in speaking of the mind of the soldier, "That God cares is never thought of—we have drifted into our present unhappy state after a time of great heedlessness to him."

When we pray, then, that God's Kingdom may come, we are praying that the total social life of man be organized with God in mind. We must concede the wide differences of opinion as to the forms of applied Christianity. But back of all these differences is this prior consideration. We may not go ahead in utter neglect of God. We are honestly trying to think his thoughts after him, and with him. This resultant realm of God is the organization of the whole of our life: home and school, trade and profession, church and state; not one of them in neglect of all the others, under God.

"Thy will be done." These words have always occasioned perplexity. If there is a God, why need we pray that his will be done, when we believe that as a matter of course it must be done?

No one has ever succeeded in squaring the rival claims of the supposed omnipotence of God and the supposed goodness of God. If God is omnipotent and at the same time good, why does he allow so much evil in the world? There is no answer to this question. We shall not find the answer that all our predecessors have missed. The truth, however, seems to be that we cannot have it both ways. And if we cannot have it both ways we had best cast our lot with the goodness of God and let the omnipotence of God take the consequences. We had best admit that there may be some things God cannot do—cannot do primarily because he has given us a genuine freedom of our own, and therefore has limited himself to that extent.

But this is really beside the mark of the prayer. We should probably be, in English, much nearer the meaning of the original words if we translated this sentence, "Thy wish be done—thy desire be done." The desire of God for mankind may be a very different thing from the omnipotent will of God operating upon us. A very devout old man I used to know once said, toward the end of his life, "The longer I live the more I am impressed by the reticence of God." That profound saying is relevant here. God's desire may be deep— beyond all our imagining—but it never invades our final freedom, and the divine reticence is an aspect of the divine desire. God is not going to overrule us, but his desires for us remain one of the determining forces of our own lives, indeed for religion it is the final force. Thus, Matthew Arnold says that the greatest single line in all poetry is the line from Dante, "In his will is our peace."

There is no proof, such as the sciences seek, for any of these statements we have been making. They are articles of faith. They are not necessarily untrue on that account.

Let me leave with you, in unequivocal words, the two options with which we are confronted. When we pray, "Our Father who art in heaven," what happens? In one of his more cynical moods Carlyle said that we stand as bewildered wanderers, "shouting question after question into the Sibyl cave of destiny, and receive no answer but an echo." Contrariwise, in one of his wisest poems Browing says:

> So through the thunder comes a human voice
> Saying, O heart I made, a heart beats here.

IX

ON KNOWING WHERE THE WIND BLOWS

Text: The wind bloweth where it listeth, and thou hearest the sound thereof, but canst not tell whence it cometh, and whither it goeth: so is every one that is born of the Spirit.—JOHN 3:8

IT has been said that man has added only two beautiful things to nature. One is the spire of a country church seen across the fields and the other is the white sails of a ship at sea. If that be so our world is much less beautiful than it was a hundred years ago because of the passing of the sailing ship.

A well-known writer, Alan Villiers, has been telling us of the dwindling fleet of the great square-rigged ships of yesterday. He makes two remarks which have a kind of parabolic value for our concerns here.

He ventures to prophesy that we may well see a return to sail, because coal and oil may become too expensive. He adds that man cannot permanently get along without the winds of heaven. So we manufacture for ourselves systems of theology and codes of ethics only to find that our machine-made religions are a heavy drain on our resources. We need some energy from outside ourselves. Religion calls this energy inspiration. The text is right in saying that we cannot control the comings and goings of this Spirit. Religion is not alone in this respect. The same is true, as countless artists have told us, in the realms of poetry, painting and music.

Indeed, looking back, one often has the feeling that the most important happenings in life have not been those which one achieved or stage-managed for oneself. They were not done by us; they were done on us. Unanticipated events befall us and alter all life thereafter. In so far as these events have turned out for our good we attribute them to what is called the grace of God. For that phrase, the grace of God, is a term which we use to describe blessings that we have not deserved and certainly have not earned by our own character and conduct. In short, religion cannot dispense with the conviction that we shall always need the winds of the Spirit.

The second thing that this writer says is, in a way, even more interesting. In one of his latest books he is describing a trip around Cape Horn in the last of the grain races from Australia to England. He says that after the ship had rounded the Horn it might very well have run into the vast calm and windless area of the South Atlantic known as the doldrums, but that the captain managed to skirt this lifeless area and keep his breeze throughout the voyage. He adds, reflectively, that if one is captain of a sailing ship it is a good thing not only to know how to handle a ship when the wind is blowing, but also to know where the winds are likely to be blowing. This is a perfectly sound footnote to the text. "The wind bloweth

where it listeth"—yes, but it is a good thing to know where to
look for that wind.

I sometimes think that we fail in our attempts to live a
Christian life because we look for religion in the wrong places,
and more particularly because we ask of religion more than it
can normally promise us. This is particularly true of our
seeking after God. We are an ambitious and impatient generation. We not only want to know all mysteries, we think
we can know them. Our advances in knowledge have been so
great that we have lost something of the intellectual modesty
of the great natural scientists of the last century and the
humility of the saints.

We need to remember what the poet says:

> Naked belief in God the omniscient, omnipotent,
> omnipresent
> Sears too much the sense of conscious creatures
> to be borne.
> That were the seeing him no flesh shall dare.

So the hymn writer says:

> Eternal Light! Eternal Light!
> How pure the soul must be,
> When, placed within Thy searching sight
> It shrinks not, but, with calm delight
> Can live, and look on Thee!

We are not that wise, and we are not that pure. Our
Protestant theology takes its first formal start with Calvin's
Institutes, and it is well to remember that Calvin said, "The
essence of God is indeed incomprehensible by us." Theology,
when it is at its best, always has held that we never see God

himself, for no man can see God and live. What we actually see is God's revelation of himself in nature, in history, in the characters of men.

Wordsworth did not argue the case for immortality, but he had nevertheless what he called intimations of immortality. What we get in much of our life is precisely such intimations of God. If we do not fail to recognize them as such and live by them they suffice us for our initiation into religion.

To return to our metaphor, then, where may we look for the winds of the Spirit?

The longer one lives and reflects on life the more convinced one is that the best values of life are always near at hand, if only we have the wit to see into things. Henry Thoreau made no public profession of religion, and he dramatized his own philosophy of life to the point of caricature. In insisting that he had the whole universe right at hand in Concord and on Walden Pond he showed great wisdom. The mode of his life, what might be called its stay-at-home quality, had affinities with the lives of Jesus, Francis of Assisi and Thomas à Kempis. The restless globe-trotting frame of mind promises little for religion. For one never can get away from oneself. That is what Augustine meant when he said, "Whither could my heart flee from my heart, and whither could I flee from myself? Whither should I not follow myself?" This is what the writer of Deuteronomy meant when he said that God's revelation "is not hidden from thee, neither is it far off. It is not in heaven, that thou shouldest say, Who shall go up for us to heaven, and bring it unto us, that we may hear it, and do it? Neither is it beyond the sea, that thou shouldest say,

Who shall go over the sea for us, and bring it unto us. . . . But the word is very nigh unto thee, in thy mouth, and in thy heart." As for the world around, we always have "stuff at hand" on which to exercise our skill.

> Not in Utopia, subterranean fields,
> Or some secreted island, Heaven knows where!
> But in the very world, which is the world
> Of all of us—the place where in the end
> We find our happiness, or not at all!

I grant you that this seems at first a rather dull and provincial account of the matter. But it is the grown-up conclusion to which most of us come. If we cannot find intimations of God in the world we know well, in our homes and friends and our day's work, we shall not be more likely to find him if we change our residence and our job and shuffle and redeal our human relationships. The wind of the Spirit blows more steadily in the world we know than it can ever blow for us in any other unknown world.

A word might be said about this place where we live and work. We are probably a very mixed congregation this morning, though our numbers are small. This is the last Sunday morning of another college year. For some of you these may be your last days in Harvard. Others of you have come back to renew the memories of past years. Still others have come to share in the festival. The rest of us live and work here, year after year.

This University is not a Y.M.C.A. nor in its totality a Divinity School, nor is it in its entirety a church. It has its own distinctive tasks to do, which bear other names. But the common charge flung at Harvard so often, that it is godless, shows very little understanding of the deeper currents of our life. Nothing, said Cardinal Newman, is easier than to use the word "God" and mean nothing by it. One often has the feeling that our pious critics may be using the name of God so easily as to mean little by it. Meanwhile, it is a very meager conception of religion which denies to the search for truth its value as one of the forms of the quest for God. And any man who knows any truth already knows something of God, even though the name of God may go unspoken. Anyone who has really come to know this University at its serious best must agree that it deserves that phrase of Royce's about The Beloved Community of Memory and Hope, and membership in such a community is an intimation of the religious life. For how shall we love God whom we have not seen, if we love not our brother whom we have seen.

But the orderliness of things as intimated to us, shall we say, by the natural sciences, leaves one question unanswered. Frederick W. H. Myers was once asked, "If you could ask the Sphinx one question and one only, what would that question be?" He replied, "If I could ask the Sphinx one question and one only and hope for an answer, I think the question would be this, 'Is the universe friendly?' "

The intimations of God which we get from much of our daily life belong in what is often called the area of natural religion. They are not the less important on that account. They are what we might call our apprenticeship in religion. The eighteenth century was quite familiar with a distinction between natural religion and revealed religion. The Catholic Church still preserves this distinction.

The Christian religion in its mature form professes to be a revealed religion. Its initial intimations are supplemented and fulfilled, in the person of Christ.

Natural religion may discover a reliable order in our universe; it leaves unanswered the problems of good and evil. Natural religion tends to be unmoral. When the devil tempts the modern mind he no longer comes in a scarlet cloak; that bit of stage property is rather worn out. He comes dressed in gray, hinting to us not that life is evil, but that it is meaningless. He suggests not that the world is hostile and unfriendly, but that it is merely indifferent.

It is at this point that Christianity takes over all prior intimations of religion with the answer to the question, "Is the universe friendly?" which it finds in the life, the teaching and the person of Jesus Christ. "For God . . . hath shined in our hearts, to give the light of the knowledge of the glory of God in the face of Jesus Christ." The winds of the Spirit are always stirring in the pages of the New Testament.

X

KEEPING THE FAITH

Text: Jesus saith unto him, Thomas, because thou hast seen me, thou hast believed: blessed are they that have not seen, and yet have believed.—JOHN 20:29

MOST of us feel a subtle difference between the first three Gospels of Matthew, Mark and Luke, and the fourth Gospel of John. Thoughtful Christians have always felt this difference. One of the Fathers of the Early Church said that Matthew, Mark and Luke were "grammatical books." He meant by these words that they are literal and historical. He then added that, by contrast, the Gospel of John is a "spiritual" work, implying that the book is not to be pressed for verbal fidelity to fact, but is a meditation long after the event on the life and teaching of Jesus, a free interpretation of Christ's work and words. It is none the less Christian on that account.

The story toward the end of John's Gospel about "Doubting Thomas" contains certain "grammatical" statements which we may find hard to accept, but it ends with the profoundly

87

"spiritual" statement which we have chosen as our text. Those who have seen believe and they are blessed. The word "blessed" literally means "fortunate." But then there are those who have not seen and yet believe, and they too are blessed. This distinction runs true to the form of many of the sayings of Jesus in the "grammatical" Gospels; it merely restates them in other words.

"Doubting Thomas" has passed into our vocabulary as a familiar figure. Indeed it might be said that every believer begins his Christian life as a "Doubting Thomas." He wants to be sure in advance of the object of his faith and the content of his faith. So much is at stake in this choice and commitment that we cannot blame him for wanting assurance in advance. Where and how is this assurance to be had?

There are three traditional answers to this question. One may simply hand over all personal responsibility for one's beliefs to an infallible church and let that church become for him the sponsor or mediator of certainty. Herein lies the historic strength and the continuing appeal of Roman Catholicism. Thus, a hundred years ago, John Henry Newman became frightened at the drift toward liberalism in the England of his day. This liberalism, a complex matter of politics, economics, morals and theology, seemed to leave him adrift in a sea that was already stormy and would become even more stormy. He did what seemed to him the only obvious thing— he dropped anchor in the Church of Rome. He says that so doing "was like coming into port after a rough sea." He prefaces the chapter in his *Apologia* which tells the tale with one of the most baffling statements in any famous autobiogra-

phy, "From the time I became a Catholic, of course I have no
further history of my religious opinions to narrate." Many
timid intellectuals in our own day have solved their problem
in this way. We are a puzzled and as a whole a tired generation. It seems a cursed spite that we should be asked to set
right these times that are so badly out of joint. Many a
modern man knows only too well what Matthew Arnold
meant, when he said

> [I am]
> Weary of myself, and sick of asking
> What I am, and what I ought to be.

It is no wonder that the confident assurance of the historic
Church of Rome has a great appeal for a certain type of
mature mind in our time and that such persons drop anchor
in its safe and landlocked harbor.

The second source of advance assurance has been traditionally sought and found by Protestants in the supposedly
infallible Bible. The greatest change made by the Reformation
was its transfer of the seat of religious authority from the
Church to the Bible. Conservative Protestant theologians have
spent infinite ingenuity in the attempt to prove that the Bible
is a uniformly consistent book, self-explanatory from cover to
cover, containing all the answers. But we know today that the
Bible is a collection of diverse and often mutually contradic-
tory books which it is sometimes hard to reconcile to one another, and which are by no means self-explanatory, either in
matters of faith or of conduct. The Bible is a marvelous book,
a self-revealing book, an inspiring book. It recapitulates for
each of us the patient experience of humanity as we relive

it in our own lives. It tells us how by long self-discipline our minds may grow up to the measure of the fullness of the stature of Christ. But even so, it leaves much to our own personal initiative and responsibility. We have to decide on our own, for instance, what it means in the terms of today to try to love our enemies. We are given the deathless principle, we are given no concrete advance account of the ways and means of applying it in our present emergency. The letter of the supposedly infallible Bible no longer solves for most of us the problem of our felt need of ethical certainty.

The third traditional source of certainty is to be found in the intimate and most inward experiences of single saintly individuals. Paul's sudden conversion on the Damascus road, Augustine's conversion in the garden at Milan, are indubitable facts which had tremendous consequences in the history of the world as well as in the private lives of the men concerned.

When Blaise Pascal died his friends found on his dead body a secret parchment worn around his neck and kept near his heart. It read in part:

> This year of Grace 1654
> Monday, November 23rd. . . .
> From about half past ten at night, to
>   about half after midnight,
>   Fire.
> God of Abraham, God of Isaac, God of Jacob,
>   Not of the philosophers and the wise.
> Security, security. Feeling, joy, peace.
>   God of Jesus Christ.
> O righteous Father, the world hath not known thee,
>   But I have known thee.
> Joy, joy, joy, tears of joy.

On the strength of those two hours Pascal went through all the rest of his life and if we may say so, that one experience "worked" for him. He was anchored on reality. Why such experiences are vouchsafed to some men and withheld from others is a psychological and moral riddle which is not easy to read.

In any case all these three types, the devout Catholic, the Fundamentalist believer in the Bible, and the single mystical saint have believed because they have seen. But there still remain the vast number of men who have not seen. I suspect that most of us belong in that group. We cannot with good conscience hand over our hunger for religious certainty to any single church, or to a book, or to the intense and solitary personal experience of the mystic which we have never shared.

I cited in my Foreword those two lines,

> Ah, what a dusty answer gets the soul,
> When hot for certainties in this our life.

These words are modern in their mood and most of us can understand them. The dread fear that life may really be meaningless is widespread today. The Tempter comes to us today, not with the seduction of the obvious scarlet vices, but rather with the insidious suggestion that life is but a tale told by an idiot, full of sound and fury, signifying nothing.

It should be said at once that this sinister thought is by no means confined to those who have never seen. This note is sounded again and again in the Bible. One of its classic statements is that in our first lesson, with the cry of Job that he had gone forward and backward, to the right hand and to the left and could not find God. He knew what it was to get the dusty answer. Jesus himself wrestled with this issue in the Garden of Gethsemane and voiced it in cry from the cross, human-all-too-human, "My God, my God, why hast thou forsaken me?"

Nothing is more clear in the witness of the saints and mystics, despite their inner assurance, to what they call the Dark Night of the Soul. To feel forsaken by God and in want of certainty has been at times their common lot. The more intimately we know good men in our own day the more aware we are that those who have seen nevertheless share in some dark hour of the night the experience of those who have never seen.

Pascal lived out a devout lifetime on the strength of the certainty vouchsafed him in those two midnight hours. But this did not mean that he could not understand and share the experience of those who have never been quite certain about it all. "I look on all sides," he says in his *Thoughts*, "and see nothing but obscurity, nature offers me nothing but matter for doubt and disquiet." (Were he living today he might say that history offers the same.) "Did I see nothing there which marked a Divinity I should decide not to believe in him. Did I see everywhere marks of a Creator I should rest peacefully in faith. But seeing too much to deny and too little to affirm, my state is pitiful, and I have a hundred times wished that if God upheld nature she would mark that fact unequivocally, but if the signs which she gives of God are fallacious, she would wholly suppress them, that she would either say all or say nothing, that I might see which part I should take."

Although Pascal was one of those who had seen, he could still understand the religious predicament of those who have not seen, and had indeed shared their dilemma.

The situation of those of us who have never seen, in the conventional terms which I have cited, seems to lead to the conclusion that religion is ultimately a matter of faith, which is a different thing from knowledge. The man who believes is the direct descendant of the father of all the faithful, Abraham, who went out into the unknown, not knowing whither he went. You may with the scientist call this act an experiment, with the explorer an adventure, or with the sportsman a deliberate gamble. After all, in entire seriousness Pascal thought of religion as the great "wager." There always is, for the religious man, "something lost behind the Ranges" and he has no option but to go and find it. Thus, again and again, we find that those who have seen, have seen only in part, and that there is yet more light to break. There are still the unseen things, and these unseen things become in the end the privilege and duty of those who have not seen.

The Christian religion makes and has always made tremendously bold affirmations about God and Christ and man and goodness and life eternal. These classic affirmations have been articles of faith and not the certainties of science. They go so far in advance of what we can prove that we may feel that we are not warranted in making them. The obvious and perhaps the intellectually respectable thing to do is to follow the example of Pontius Pilate, to wash one's hands of them and have nothing to do with them, to lapse into a respectable agnosticism. But somehow this wise procedure has always seemed to me, in Browning's words, an "evasion of life's proof." And in these moments, invaded by the inevitable perplexities which attend the act of faith, I have tried to imagine myself pledging my life to the defense of an out-and-out anti-Christian interpretation of life and the world. I have been much reassured to find that other men, such as the late Bishop Hensley Henson, have also pondered that alternative.

St. Paul says that Christians are the stewards of their religion. L. P. Jacks has substituted the word "trustees." Most of us can get fresh heart and peace of mind in these days if we can learn to think of ourselves as trustees of Christianity. That familiar hymn "Rock of Ages Cleft for Me" was translated years ago into Hindustani for use in missions in India. When literally translated back into the English the Indian text reads, "A very old stone split for my special benefit." Far too many Christians think of their religion in just those terms, a very old set of ideas devised for their special benefit. Each of us needs and ought to get private reassurance from his faith. But that is not his whole nor probably his most important relation to his religion. He is, in these troubled days, not so much a beneficiary of Christianity as its steward, its trustee. He owes it to his times and to future times to administer his trusteeship with good conscience and not to regard its capital as a private fund which he may spend solely upon himself. He ought to be able to say of his discipleship, "I have kept the faith," not for my own personal satisfaction, but for the helping of the world. That, then, is the opportunity of those blessed and even fortunate Christians of our own times who have not seen and yet have believed.

XI

THE TRANSMUTING OF EVIL

Text: For [wisdom] will walk with him by crooked ways, and
. . . torment him with her discipline, until she may trust his soul,
and try him by her laws. Then will she return the straight way unto
him, and comfort him, and shew him her secrets.
—ECCLESIASTICUS 4:17, 18

THE Bible as a whole has a tremendous sense of motion.
Human life is described as a journey. The Bible therefore
makes constant use of the word "way." It gives us a kind of
road map of life with both the directions and the gradients.

In the text the Bible contrasts two kinds of ways which we
meet in the journey of life: the straight way and the crooked
way. The prophets were always promising that the crooked
ways of the world should be made straight, but they never
found it easy to redeem those promises. The men of the Bible
lived in a semimountainous land and in such lands the road
winds uphill all the way.

The contrast between the crooked ways and the straight

ways raises, of course, the stubborn problem of evil. It has been said that we call those things good which require no explanation, and those things evil which do not explain themselves. Why is not the face of nature and history like our own Great Plains where the roads run straight and level mile after mile? Why is the face of things so uneven that we have to travel by crooked roads?

These crooked roads of life are of two kinds. There are those which are forced on us, whether we will or no, by the contours of nature itself or the shape of history. We have to travel them, but they are not of our own making. Then there are the crooked paths which we make for ourselves. As the old verse has it: "All we like sheep have gone astray. We have turned every one to his own way."

There are at least three possible ways of dealing with the fact of evil, whether imposed upon us, or done by us. No one of these solutions is fully satisfying, but each is a practical method of dealing with the situation.

We may take the position of the absolute idealist, from St. Augustine to Mary Baker Eddy, and say that evil is not real; only the good is real. Therefore, we simply try to stare evil out of countenance.

We may say that evil has been put there for us to fight against and thus train ourselves morally. It is the baby's teething ring and the pugilist's punching bag. Like Lincoln, in his attitude toward slavery, we are to hit it and hit it hard.

Or we may say that evil is stubbornly actual and must be fought with, but once it is overcome it can be turned to good account. By moving it around in the equation of life we may finally change its signs from negative to positive. Thus we say to the bit of crooked road along which we may be finding our way, "I will not let thee go, except thou bless me." We might call this the dramatic solution of the problem of evil.

That such a solution is possible is beyond dispute. William Wordsworth in his youth and early manhood traveled over some very crooked ways, many of them imposed on him by the fortunes of the French Revolution, others fashioned for himself by his own waywardness. Eventually, looking back on these crooked ways, when he had at last found a straight way, back home in his beloved Lake District, he said,

> There is a dark
> Inscrutable workmanship that reconciles
> Discordant elements, makes them cling together
> In one society. How strange that all
> The terrors, pains and early miseries,
> Regrets, vexations, lassitudes interfused
> Within my mind, should e'er have borne a part,
> And that a needful part, in making up
> The calm existence that is mine when I
> Am worthy of myself.

This is something more than the promise which Vergil gave his wanderer Aeneas that perhaps, at some later time, it may be a pleasure to look back on the hardships through which one has passed. It is St. Paul's promise that for a good man all things can be made to work together for good. This is the distinctively Christian way of dealing with life's crooked ways. It is a subtle doctrine and liable to abuse. One remembers the rather weak and sentimental man who said of himself that he belongs to "The Little Church of Those Who Stumble and Rise Again." He allowed himself the pleasure of stumbling for the sake of the even more pleasurable remorse which followed when he rose again. St. Paul says that this is what one may not do. One may not sin in order that grace may abound.

In this season of Lent, 1950, we admit to ourselves that we do have to travel by crooked ways, especially those which we make for ourselves. And I venture to suggest that we try to think of these experiences in a Christian spirit.

We Americans are a prodigally, even a wickedly wasteful people; wasteful of our natural resources, wasteful of our food, wasteful of time and money. Few of us waste the good experiences of life, many of us probably waste most of the harder experiences of life, those that we labeled evil when we were passing through them. These may be our failures, our pains, our sorrows, even our sins. Our instinct is to forget all such events, seal them up in the tomb of lost memories, and get on to the next thing. That attempt is psychologically impossible and probably psychologically dangerous.

William Wordsworth died just a hundred years ago this spring. This centennial has been the occasion for a good many persons to turn back to that neglected poet. Just after the death of his first wife, Leslie Stephen once wrote a fine critical essay on Wordsworth's ethics. Stephen's biographer, Maitland, says of this essay that it was a lay sermon which Stephen preached to himself on the unselfish use of sorrow. Sorrow comes to all of us, perhaps rather later than earlier in his life, but it is a universal experience. In any case Stephen says in his essay, "All moral teaching, I have sometimes fancied, might be summed up in the one formula, 'Waste not.' The waste of sorrow is one of the most lamentable forms of waste. Sorrow is deteriorating so far as it is selfish. But it may, if rightly used, serve only to detach us from the lower motives and give sanctity to the higher." All this is based upon that penetrating line of Wordsworth's in which he speaks of "the power an agonizing sorrow to transmute." At that point the poet was intuitively Christian, though he does not use church words.

The noblest instance which I know of in this connection is an incident reported in Trevelyan's life of John Bright. Years after the event, at the unveiling of a statue of Richard Cobden at Bradford, Bright told of a visit which he had had from Cobden just after his, Bright's wife, had died.

> On the day when Mr. Cobden called upon me I was in the depths of grief, I might almost say of despair. Mr. Cobden called upon me as my friend and addressed to me words of condolence. After a time he looked up and said, "There are thousands of homes in England at this moment where wives, mothers, and children are dying of hunger. Now, when the first paroxysm of your grief is past, I would advise you to come with me and we will never rest until the Corn Law is repealed."

A devout layman, who was by no means a formal Christian, once wrote an essay on the doctrine of the atonement. The basis of that doctrine, he said, is the conviction, which may be verified in the life of any one of us, that an experience of the evil which is in the world may become the occasion for a greater good than otherwise would ever have happened. Off the record he once told a friend that this formulation of the doctrine of the atonement had been suggested to him by a woman who had told him her story. She was a delicate, sensitive person who had for years been married to a sensual and brutal husband who had subjected her to countless indignities and shame. In due time he died and she was left with the wreck of her life on her hands. She decided not to waste her experience and opened up a quiet home for prostitutes. She felt and felt rightly that she could at least understand the humiliating and degrading experiences through which they, too, had passed. It goes without saying that she was of incalculable help to those women off the street. She restored them not merely to decent ways of life, but to an ultimate self-respect.

This principle and process of transmuting the agonizing sorrows of life need not be restricted to sorrow itself, or to shame. It is capable of translation and application to all of our experiences along the crooked ways of life. These experiences may help us mature our own characters, as in Wordsworth's case. But their ultimate meaning is more than that. They increase our powers of sympathy, and of all the healing, helpful powers in life that of sympathy is the greatest. So, I remember a minister's wife who once said to me the day after her husband had died, "All my life I have been trying to comfort people in sorrow and now I realize that I didn't know the least thing about it." We do well to consider, therefore, what might be called the unselfish use of our experiences along the crooked ways of life.

Beyond one's own maturing character and such help as one may give to those with whom one comes in touch, lie the major political and moral problems of our time. These are of

13023
such complexity and gravity that they seem altogether to
overshadow what happens to oneself.

Our world has been traveling through very crooked ways
for thirty years and more. The cynic says that history teaches
only one thing, in that it teaches nothing. But it is time that
we began to learn something from history. One may hesitate
to lapse into cynicism and as an individual one often feels
pathetically helpless. Yet it often seems as though all the hard
experiences along the crooked ways of the two wars has been
pretty much wasted by our generation.

Yet one cannot fail to note a change in the air we breathe.
The conscience of thoughtful people is becoming troubled
about the possible future. Preachers are usually written off and
discounted because they are subsidized to repeat moral
platitudes. But military men and scientists are wondering
themselves about the morality of the next proposed steps in
the development of the apparatus for war. On their own
account they are asking whether such projects may not go
against the moral grain of the American people. Unless I
entirely misread the facts there are a great many individuals,
who, as far as they privately and personally are concerned,
would prefer to be destroyed by the next bomb rather than
to assume the moral responsibility of killing other persons by
the same means. This would be in fact a hideously difficult
decision to make, because such a decision would involve not
merely oneself, but one's family and friends and thousands of
one's fellow citizens. Nevertheless, there is no question about
the widespread and deeply troubled conscience of serious

people. That disquiet will not be settled too cheaply nor too easily.

Mr Winston Churchill has never been a very pious or preachy man. His suggestion that we should again make an honest attempt to try to get through the Iron Curtain and at the Kremlin may be doomed to disappointment from the first. It would be risky, but so is the alternative. In any case it is a very ungenerous judgment to dismiss his proposal as a shrewd electioneering stunt prompted merely by party politics. It is not for us to sit in judgment on his sincerity or dismiss him as a political opportunist. We can only consent to his blunt words that the Christian religion would seem to demand of us every such effort at reconciliation with our adversary, whatever the outcome of that effort. Otherwise, the waste of the hard experiences of all these years will be the real tragedy of our times. And otherwise, we shall wander in ways that become ever more crooked with no sight of any straight way ahead.

XII

LOSING LIFE AND FINDING IT

Text: He that findeth his life shall lose it: and he that loseth his life for my sake shall find it.—MATTHEW 10:39

ON one of his forced marches in the heart of darkest Africa, Henry M. Stanley found himself faced with starvation. He said that at such a time something ugly appears in the mind like the head of a tortoise coming out from under its shell. When men become hungry, the white man is only twenty-four hours ahead of the black man and both of them only forty-eight hours ahead of the cannibal.

We are quite familiar today with this account of human nature. We know that the unconscious mind is a repository for all kinds of thrusts from our animal ancestry, from primitive racial memories, and from elemental prenatal sensations.

This popular account of our mental underworld is rather depressing. Down there the ape and the tiger, the primeval savage and the gangster are plotting against our decency and sanity. It is worth pointing out in passing that the newer

103

sciences of the mind have given fresh life to the old doctrine of original sin. Human nature is apparently by no means as ideal and lovely an affair as we formerly supposed it to be.

In religion this dread of our own underworld has taken away something of our sense of inner security. We used to say that, however hard and hostile the outer world may be, there is an impregnable inner world where there is quiet and peace and security. Now, most of us wonder whether this is true. For Dr. Jung tells us that if a man "turns away from the terrifying prospect of a blind world around him and turns inward upon the recesses of his own mind, he will discover there chaos and darkness. Science has destroyed the refuge of the inner life. What was once a sheltering haven has become a place of terror."

No one of us can deny a measure of truth in this account of our total make-up. But one cannot help feeling that, in the attempt to make his case, Jung has overstated it. This whole account of the evil role which the unconscious mind plays in our lives is at best a half truth. Therefore, it is occasionally worth while to state the other half truth just as bluntly. For, if many of our deeper memories and thrusts are a moral liability, so there is also in that same underworld a racial treasury of merits which is a moral asset. In short, even a modern, intelligent Christian need not despair of the inner man. And it is part of the business of education and religion to state the positive side of the case for our deeper life.

Let me give two illustrations, the first from the field of education. The name of William James, who was teaching at Harvard fifty years ago, is known to many. I think that the

finest tribute I have ever heard paid to any teacher anywhere
was paid to James by one of his students. He said, "You went
to other men's lectures here at Harvard and you were impressed, even oppressed, by the lecturer's massive learning, by
his greatness as a scholar. But you never came out of James'
lecture room feeling what a great man James is. You came out
with a strange new thought and feeling, 'If I could only find
myself, what a great man I might be.'"

The other illustration, this time from religion, comes from
the life of a quiet little clergyman in the East End of London,
Samuel Barnett. He put this placard outside his church of
St. Jude's in Whitechapel, "There is a poem on the 'Buried
Life' of which I am often reminded. Your lives are busy and
useful, but your faces are anxious and you are not all you
want to be. There is within you another life which does not
get free. Men carry about a buried life. I believe that in a
quiet place we may wait God's call. St. Jude's Church will be
open on Sunday evenings. Will you come in for even ten
minutes. It may be that as you listen to the silence or the
music God will speak, that the buried life will arise and that
you will have peace." That simple invitation has always
seemed to me to state the real reason for going to church.

In short, religion and education are entitled to believe that
there still is such a thing in the mind as a "central peace subsisting at the heart of endless agitation." Education and religion are both warranted in believing that when the deeper
mind asserts itself it is not necessarily a Pandora's box out of
which troubles and deviltries come, but that there is also what
the poet calls an "imprisoned splendor" in each of us and that

learning and worshiping are a matter of finding "a way for the imprisoned splendor to escape."

Now if it be true, and I think it is true, that in the deeper self there is not only a sinister self, but also a better self than we now know, the question arises how to discover and release that self. One thing is clear. We cannot find our buried, better self, if one may say so, by fishing for it. None of the processes of introspection will get at it. It will come to the surface of conscious life only in response to the appeal of some imperious reality around us in nature, or history, or art, or human affection. Thus a Boston surgeon, Dr. Benjamin Tenney, once said, "It has taken me half my life to discover that my business in the world is not to try to make something of myself, but rather to find a job worth doing and lose myself in it." That is a homely way of saying what in substance Jesus said, "He that would save his present self will lose that self, but he who can lose the self he now knows will find a self he had not known or even suspected." So a sophisticated, self-conscious young man responded years ago to the summons of World War I, "Now God be thanked who has matched us with this hour."

You will remember that Emerson used to say, "When the half gods go, the whole gods come." Our fathers thought they had found the whole gods, and up to a point perhaps they had. What is commonly called the loss of religion today is largely a matter of the disappearance of our ancestral whole gods. Emerson's process has been reversed and now we have to say, "When the whole gods go, the half gods come." Qualitatively there is still a great deal of religion left in the modern

world; the difficulty is that it is a religion of the half gods.
The gods of race, of blood, of state, of class, have been for the
last thirty or forty years served with fanatical zeal. And a
lukewarm devotion to ancestral whole gods is a very poor
substitute for passionate devotion to some tribal or political
or economic half god. Many of our moral and spiritual problems today arise from that fact.

One realizes that the Christian religion, in the form in
which so many of us know and practice it, is not getting a fair
chance at us because we are fighting to keep some fragments of
a superficial self that will have to be let go if we are ever to
release the deeper, better self. We all know this to be true of
ourselves. It is not fair to blame Christianity; the trouble
is with us.

> 'Tis ye, 'tis ye,
> 'Tis your estranged faces
> That miss the many splendored thing.

Our text comes in the first instance from the Gospels. By
now everyone knows the name of Albert Schweitzer, some
know a good deal about him as a theologian, a philosopher, a
musician, a doctor. His history and example arouse comment
and criticism. At any rate, he is not the sort of man who can
be ignored. Opinions about him vary. A liberal clergyman in
Los Angeles wrote recently in a leading religious journal, "Am
I the only American clergyman who finds Schweitzer, for all
his medical work in Africa, and for all his scholarship a
defeatist, a pessimist about progress, a man in retreat from the
work of democracy in the world? I find something of the

imperialist in his attitudes toward the Negro people of the
Congo and something of a Spengler in his hopelessness about
civilization. Am I wrong?" In my own opinion it would be
impossible in the seven lines quoted to be more wrong.

After lecturing at the Goethe Centennial in Colorado in
July, 1949, Schweitzer stopped in Cambridge and spent one
day with us at Harvard. We put on no special ceremonies
for him. We merely let him do what he wanted most to do,
have a free day playing our organs. He spent the first part of
the morning at the Skinner organ factory in Dorchester, going
over the new organ being built for Symphony Hall, and then
he came out to us. He played the organ in our church for an
hour and then went on for another hour to play the baroque
organ in the Germanic museum.

The immediate experience and now the memory of that day
stands out as one of the two or three really great days over
the long years which I have spent in the University. The one
obvious, imperious fact about the man was his absolute
unself-consciousness. Whatever is meant by childlikeness and
entering the Kingdom of God as a little child, Schweitzer has
it and he is it. He would probably have been just the same over
a text of the Gospels or an operating table. Here it happened
to be our organs. There was not a hint of the virtuoso dis-
playing his talents, not even the slightest interest in whether
we were listening and enjoying his music; only utter absorp-
tion, first in the mechanism of the organs and then in the
music of Bach which he played. He made you feel rather
shabby and superficial. You realized that he had gone much
further into the mysteries of art and science and religion than

you had gone. Whatever life is for, and whatever the universe is like, you had some intimation of these things as you watched him at our organs. He had found that self which ought to be the true self of every man, because he had had the moral courage and the spiritual vision to lose the superficial self with which we all start life.

Schweitzer is a Christian. He is not a conventional or orthodox Christian, but he has done what he has done and is what he is because he thinks his way of life is what Christ asks of his followers today. He cannot be explained on any secular grounds.

I am minded in conclusion to hark back to a sonnet of Matthew Arnold's on this problem of losing and finding oneself. It is applicable to Schweitzer; it would have been equally applicable to Samuel Barnett at St. Jude's in East London. It might be applicable—it ought to be—to any one of us who professes and calls himself a Christian.

> 'Twas August, and the fierce sun overhead
> Smote on the squalid streets of Bethnal Green,
> . . . .
> I met a preacher there I knew, and said:
> "Ill and o'erworked, how fare you in this scene?"
> "Bravely!" said he; "for I of late have been
> Much cheer'd by thoughts of Christ, *the living bread.*"
>
> O human soul! so long as thou canst so
> Set up a mark of everlasting light,
> Above the howling senses' ebb and flow,
> To cheer thee, and to right thee if thou roam—
> Not with lost toil thou labourest through the night!
> Thou mak'st the heaven thou hop'st indeed thy home.

XIII

A WORLD WITHOUT CHRIST

Text: From that time many of his disciples went back, and walked no more with him.

Then said Jesus unto the twelve, Will ye also go away?

Then Simon Peter answered him, Lord, to whom shall we go? thou hast the words of eternal life.—JOHN 6:66-68

THERE is a phrase coined by one of our number some years ago which has now passed into our vernacular about "The Beloved Community of Memory and Hope." Those words of Royce can never become so shop soiled that they lose their majesty and meaning. Behind and beneath and beyond all our daily give and take is the awareness, "I belong here," and one never comes to the time when one says, "I used to belong here." One will always say, "I belong here."

This is in other terms a description of our relation to our religion. However faithful or unfaithful, however wayward and forgetful, we belong to it. Once having belonged the world cannot take that experience away from us. Thus there is a brief and lovely injunction to Timothy of long ago in a

110

letter written to him by an older Christian friend, "Remember Jesus Christ." Little else is said. Timothy was left with his own traditional memories of Christ and his interpretation of the life he should live with those memories in mind.

There is a theory that in its first and purest days Christianity was so simple a matter that no one could possibly misunderstand it. Supposedly it had no unnecessary complications. But this is a false reading of the text. Even his first disciples often misunderstood Jesus. The simple things in life are always the hardest to understand, that is, to understand fully. And when understanding means applying them to everyday conduct they are by no means so simple as they seem. Thus Christianity from the first was, as it has been ever since, a matter of divided opinions and of much practical perplexity. The most and the best any Christian can do in the presence of these perplexities is not to think of them in their own terms, but to try to get the premise for the whole riddle by harking back to Paul's injunction to Timothy, "Remember Jesus Christ.' For there are ways of thinking about life and modes of action which are felt to be out of bounds when one remembers Jesus Christ.

One of the more sobering and saddening things about our American life is the dwindling part which Christianity plays in the conduct of our public affairs. One wonders how often in the strife of tongues which has been going on in Washington the name of God and the name of Christ have been cited. Citations of that sort are usually rather an embarrassment to all concerned. They certainly are not taken for granted as the rock on which our house is builded. And when some states-

man quotes one of the more gentle words of Jesus he is liable
to be rebuked as either a mere dreamer or a potential traitor.
In any case breaches of taste of this sort are pronounced bad
strategy politically.

Let it be said at once in defense of the state that the
churches themselves are in part to blame for the increasing
anticlericalism on the part of the state. The Christian Church
is by law established in England and the Archbishop of
Canterbury lives in Lambeth Palace in London. Someone
asked the late William Temple what were the political rights
and duties of the Church of England. He said, "It is the office
of Lambeth to remind Westminster of its duty to God."
There is no such palace in Washington and it would be an
impertinence for any one churchman to assume that he is
constitutionally authorized to remind Congress of its duty to
God. But churches are becoming pushful in these days. Some
of them have their own political lobbies. Some of them nur-
ture secret dreams of becoming an American established
church. In defense of the equal rights of all churches before
the law, the state finds itself forced more and more into a
neutral position which can only be described as a studied
and deliberate secularity. It must stand apart and take no
sides unless the laws of the land are violated or invoked
by litigants. It is, therefore, a fair question how far America
may be called a Christian country. T. S. Eliot is probably
right in contending that a country may be said to be Christian
until it has officially declared itself to be something else. We
are to this extent more Christian than Nazi Germany was or
Communist Russia and its satellites now are. You and I can
worship here in accordance with our religious convictions,

without being noted by state police at the door and liable thereafter to prison or slave labor camps. We probably can never realize how great our freedom is until it is challenged or denied. And happily we can see no prospect of that sort on our political horizon. Yet we are aware that what we think and say and do here has little direct effect upon the conduct of the affairs of state.

What, therefore, is the relation of our religion to the land and the times in which we live? A famous Danish thinker, Harald Höffding, said some years ago that formerly Christianity was the pillar of cloud by day and of fire by night which marched in the vanguard of history, but that now it is only an ambulance corps trailing along in the rear of the conflict caring for the sick and wounded. That is a fairly accurate account of the world-wide situation in so far as nominally Christian states are concerned. This verdict would appear to be an adverse comment upon the importance of Christianity in the modern world—its relegation, to reverse Browning's words, "from the dreadful van to the safe glad rear." Personally I have always felt that those words were an indictment and dismissal of the whole medical profession. To put it bluntly, Are you willing to live in a world where there are no doctors? Unimpaired health is a rare and brief experience in human life. We all need healing help. Both medicine and religion know that good physicians of body and soul are a necessary part of our lives. Even if religion and medicine do not make military and political policies in the dreadful van of history, they know how to live and what to do in a world where man is born to trouble as the sparks fly upward.

Furthermore, there is another comment to be made on that

remark of the Danish scholar. There have been, it is true, ages when religion marched in the vanguard of history. These are called the great ages of faith. But those ages will not bear too much close moral examination. They were the ages of fanaticism, of bigotry, and often of cruelty. Their supposed religious vanguard was often little better than a caricature of Christianity. Such religion as they had was invoked to seem to give spiritual sanction to worldly interests. Power can corrupt churchmen, as well as statesmen, and there have been many historic churchmen in the vanguard of history who have been all but absolutely corrupted. In self-defense of our ambulance corps, which is at least among men as one who serves, we have a right not to regret unduly the passing of the ages when religion seemed to be the maker of history, at the head of the procession. There is much truth in Dean Inge's remark that the church like some political parties has always done well in opposition and badly in power. Thus the Christ whom we would remember will probably become less a crusader clad in armor charging into action and more the good Samaritan kneeling by the roadside to minister to the victim of the world's highwaymen. It is he who stoops to conquer.

I recall that familiar story, *The Man without a Country*. It is the tale of a young naval officer who in a moment of anger said that he hoped he might never hear of the United States again. The court before which he had been brought said that this should be his punishment. He was kept aboard one ship after another the rest of his life, transferred from one vessel which was approaching America as another was leaving. He never saw his country again, he was never allowed even to hear of it. All mention of it was cut out of papers he saw, no one ever mentioned it in his presence. The folly of his hot desire only dawned on him as the years went on.

There were times in his own life when his contemporaries wished Jesus had never crossed their path. He complicated life; he raised questions which were hard to answer. They besought him to depart out of their cities. The rich young ruler turned away sorrowful because he had great possessions and Christ asked too much.

There is a theory abroad that a great surge of new hunger for religion is sweeping through our world. I wonder is this really so, or if it is so can it be trusted? Is it unfair to say that what most people want is some snap cure for their troubles and some guarantee of security, and that neither of these can now be had soon or easily or cheaply. Jesus might still say what he said to some of his own disciples, "Ye know not what ye ask."

There are times in one's own life when one becomes really aware of the inexorable and austere demands which Christianity ought to make on us. And so there are times when, in a way, we wish Christ would depart out of our world, when indeed we wish that we had never known him. For we have great possessions—not money so much—but involvement in a vast semipagan social structure which has many interests other than those that made the mind of Christ.

But suppose now that history and miracle were suddenly to take us at our word. Suppose this figure of Christ were to be absolutely effaced and wiped out of the world. Gone from our literature, gone from our art, gone from our music and much of it our very best music, gone from all the ministries of help and healing, gone from Molokai, gone from Lambaréné, utterly and finally gone, so that we should never even hear the name again. Well, most of us, however little we realize it now, would be men without a country, without a homeland of the human soul. We should not know or understand even the world we would be living in, much less any other world which we can only call spiritual and eternal.

When most of his fellow countrymen were falling away from him, Jesus turned and asked Peter, "Will ye also go away?" That question was asked in all seriousness; it was not a rhetorical question. One gets the impression that for a moment Peter felt its force and was not sure what his answer should be. But second thought prompted him in all seriousness to say, "Lord, to whom shall we go? thou hast the words of eternal life."

It is in some such sober spirit, thinking long, long thoughts, that we ponder over our own lives in these times. As far as we can see there is no promising or enduring alternative to the Christian religion when it is true to itself. A world which is to last and a nation which is to be stable cannot permanently dispense with those attitudes, tempers and deep emotions which are for us incarnate in the person of Christ. A world which jettisons them is headed for self-destruction.

Therefore, it is very right and proper that those of us who profess and call ourselves Christians should, at this time and in this Beloved Community of Memory and Hope, try again to fulfill the old injunction to Timothy. "Remember Jesus Christ."

XIV

THE LORD'S SONG IN A STRANGE LAND
A Sermon for Thanksgiving Day

Text: How shall we sing the Lord's song in a strange land?
—Psalm 137:4

O F all the festivals which man has observed that of the harvest is probably the oldest and the most universal. Man may have planted and tended his crops, but he knows that it is the earth that has given the increase. It has been reckoned that to the making of the full corn in the ear man may have contributed 5 per cent; while the earth has given 95 per cent. In so far as we believe that the earth is not a happy accident in nature, but is itself the creation of God, the humble human admission that for life we are dependent upon God and the consequent expression of gratitude to God are a a right and proper instinct.

Conversely, of all the chronic sins of humanity that of taking things for granted, and thus of ingratitude, is one of the most common. It was said of Jesus that he needed not that any should tell him of man, for he knew what was in man. But even Jesus was puzzled by the thanklessness of man. Of the ten lepers whom he healed only one lingered to give thanks to God, and Jesus asked in honest perplexity, "Were there not ten cleansed? but where are the nine?"

The observance of Thanksgiving Day in our America in these years would be, and is, an honest attempt to avoid the sin of ingratitude. We are living, and we are among the few peoples of the world so living, in a land of comfort and plenty. We have lived in such a land so long that we take it for granted. But it is well worth our while to pause for a moment to remember that it is by no means of our desert that we can so live. When we look abroad over the widespread world of hunger and naked want we shall do well to say, "There but for the grace of God go I," and to pass on to the moral awareness that to whom much is given of him shall much be required.

Thanksgiving Day was from the first, and particularly here in Massachusetts, something more than a routine harvest festival. Even in the Plymouth of the 1620's it concerned the whole venture of the prophetic Pilgrim society. It had social, historical and religious overtones. And it is these overtones which give to the day much of its continuing meanings. The Founding Fathers of the Republic subsequently divorced church and state. The tendency to separate the two has grown on us greatly in most recent years. The reluctance of the state to concede the relevance of that for which the church stands is one of the major ethical dilemmas of the present time. But however effectively the state may keep the modern church out of the conduct of its affairs, is can never divorce citizenship from religion. The importance of the observance of Thanksgiving Day, in these years, lies in no small part in the concession on the part of the state that this is so. The day is one of the two or three occasions in the year when church and state concede that which they have in common.

The Pilgrim Fathers were not the discoverers of America. This continent had already been known for a hundred and thirty years before the *Mayflower* dropped anchor in Provincetown harbor. In 1614 Captain John Smith had coasted along these shores and mapped them. Before ever the Pilgrims landed he gave their place names to Cape Elizabeth, and Cape Ann, to the Charles River and indeed to Plymouth itself. But he had brought back to England a discouraging report of what he had found. In memorable words he said that he was not so simple as to suppose that any motive other than riches would ever erect here a commonwealth or draw company from their ease and humors at home to stay in New England. Therefore, John Fiske adds, "It was left for religious enthusiasm to achieve what commercial enterprise failed to accomplish."

The *Mayflower* rounded the tip of Cape Cod on November 11, 1620. The Pilgrims' first view of these shores confirmed the report which Captain Smith had brought back to England. In the memorable words of Governor Bradford, "What could they see but a hideous and desolate wilderness, full of wild beasts and wild men? For summer being done, all things stand upon them with a weatherbeaten face; and the whole country represented a wild and savage hue."

The story of their first costly winter at Plymouth, when half their number were laid away on Burial Hill, is familiar. The gathering in of their first precarious harvest was the occasion for the first Thanksgiving Day. Had they not been, as Bradford adds, men who were not easily discouraged, and had they not been sustained by an indomitable faith in God, their settlement would have gone the way of prior commercial ventures up and down the coast which had previously been planted and then abandoned. I know of no verse in the Bible which comes as near the truth of their venture as that of our text. Their problem was to learn how to sing the Lord's song in a strange land.

That problem in the terms in which they first met it, they solved. They solved it for themselves and so doing they solved it for their descendants. The first seven years in Plymouth were, it is true, a near thing; they were touch and go. But by 1627 the Plymouth Colony had taken sufficient root on this soil so that the subsequent exodus to Massachusetts Bay had warrant and precedent in the achieved fact of Plymouth. They did it once for all. Never since that day has there been any question as to the ability of man to maintain life on this continent.

But I have said these things as a reminder that the problem which the Pilgrims faced is forever being restated. This vast continent was explored and conquered over the following two hundred years. The ancient westward thrust of the human race, starting centuries before in the steppes of Asia, came full circle when we reached the Pacific Ocean. After that there was no farther west to which man might go. For more than a hundred years now the mind of America has had to turn back upon itself to consolidate its culture.

To put it in its simplest terms, the day has never come, and it is doubtful whether it ever can come, when the single individual will not find himself asking, if he has been a religious person, how he shall go on singing the Lord's song in what is to him a strange land which he had never anticipated and for which he is unprepared. The chances and changes of this mortal life confront each one of us with emergencies that test the validity of his personal religion. If that religion is dependent upon some too familiar soil and cannot be transplanted into new soil, a man loses his religion. It is a fair question whether that which he loses has deserved the name of religion. For living religion is a powerful energy capable of reasserting itself under new and untried circumstance. None of us can ever be sure that he has a religion until it has been proved in some strange land. A faith which withers and dies in that land is not the Christian religion.

Beyond all this there is the problem of the strange lands into which history is leading our people. The pastures and the hillsides and the plains of America have been brought under fruitful control. They have yielded their harvest this year as for years past.

But if we think back over American life as a whole and then think of it as it is today, we cannot help feeling that as a people we have been and still are moving into strange lands. For two centuries and a half we believed ourselves to be living a self-sufficient national life, the rest of the world forgetting and by that world forgot. Since the days of the Pilgrims there has not been a citizen in this land who did not come here himself or in the person of his forebears because life in the Old World had been economically, politically or religiously intolerable. We are a nation of refugees. This is what makes it so hard for Europeans to understand us and for us to understand them.

It is hard to say when the settled habit and the formal faith of isolationism began to be changed. Perhaps with the Spanish-American War, which left us with a duty in the Philippines. Certainly with World War I and more certainly with World War II. The last fifty years have brought America into strange lands for which its previous history had given it no preparation. The remaking of our minds has been painful and tedious and costly.

For those of us who profess and call ourselves Christians the problem still remains, how to sing the Lord's song in these strange lands, strange racially and economically and politically. A generation ago we still dreamed of what was then called a return to normalcy. Rude events have wakened us from that pleasant dream. No thoughtful man really believes that there is any such return. It is as though we heard a voice from Sinai telling us that we have lingered long enough by the mountain of past years; we must strike our tents and move on.

The problem of the Lord's song in a strange land is no longer stated in the homely terms of primitive Plymouth, but it is restated in the imperative terms of our own day. Our Christianity is, therefore, being put to the old test in new terms. We cannot say that it is so absolutely identified with any political party, or any church polity, or any particular economic status. We have no assurance of the immortality in history of any of these old and familiar facts. Whether we will or no we have to make our peace with the fact that we are living through one of the periods of radical change in the structure of society. Unless our American Protestant Christianity has today the inner vitality of historic Christianity, which has survived all such changes down the centuries, we shall indeed lose our religion. For each of us this is a solitary spiritual discipline, wrought out, perhaps, in the lonely watches of the night, when we make our mental and moral peace with the kind of world in which we are living and shall continue to live as long as we shall live. The question which Thanksgiving Day puts to us is, "How shall we sing the Lord's song in a strange land."

Let me end with a remark made to me a few years ago by one of Harvard's most distinguished professors, Arthur Edwin Kennelly. He was nearly blind; his wife was dying of a painful disease in an upper room of the home where I had called to see him. I tried to say something intimate about this world which was closing in around that home. He brushed all that aside, and as I parted from him he said, "We ought to be profoundly thankful for having been allowed to live at so great a time as this." In his blindness and with pain all about him and sorrow awaiting him he was singing the Lord's song in a strange land.

XV

GOD WITH US
A Christmas Sermon

Text: They shall call his name Emmanuel, which being interpreted is, God with us.—Matthew 1:23

THE *Mayflower* dropped anchor in Plymouth harbor on December 21, 1620. Therefore, our Pilgrim Fathers were hardly in a position to celebrate Christmas that year. The record says, of their first Christmas in New England, "We went on shore, some to fell tymber, some to saw, some to rive, and some to carry, so that no man rested all that day."

One might have supposed that things would have been better a year later. But in his *History of the Plimmeth Plantation* Governor Bradford concludes his record of the year 1621 by saying, "On the day called Christmas-day, the Governor called them out to work as was usual." For many years thereafter Pilgrims and Puritans studiously avoided any recognition of Christmas whatsoever. They said that it was a pagan and popish festival in which they would have no part. What they objected to was the last syllable in the word Christmas, with its suggestion that it was the day on which a mass is said in Christ's honor.

It was a long time before our New England churches grudgingly admitted Christmas into the calendar for the church year.

Between then and now the day has become the most familiar of all our holidays. The life of our homes, the programs of our schools and colleges, the shrewd organization of our trade have all been geared to this day for weeks in advance and then for weeks in retrospect.

Culturally we Americans live by overstatement. Somehow we do not seem able to do a thing like Christmas without overdoing it. The result is that thousands upon thousands of persons in this country, for reasons altogether other than those which prompted Governor Bradford, would be glad to see the whole season go unobserved. They are the weary shopgirls, the overburdened postmen, the worn-out drivers of delivery vans, the distracted grocers and butchers and florists. Thus a clerk said to me recently, "I am so tired I cannot even add up the figures on your bill." All that such persons ask is to sleep the clock around from Christmas Eve to Christmas night. Whatever may be said in defense of our kind of Christmas, it has become a poor vehicle for anything like a sensitive humanitarianism.

Yet, in spite of all this, there is something, indeed very much, to be said for the continued observance of Christmas, as against the strong strain of an almost pagan overstatement.

In the first place, stated festivals are a necessary part of ongoing life. For life today, perhaps more than ever in days that are gone, tends to be fragmented. The wild chaos of our times seems to be driven by a kind of centrifugal energy. We are left with bits of the self, bits of our world, bits of history which have little in common. A major mental problem is how to make these disparate fragments of experience cohere. Emily Dickinson within the four walls of her garden in Amherst knew this and struggled to keep at heel that Single Hound which is the soul's identity.

The stated private festivals of a home on its intimate anniversaries, the public festivals of church and state are, therefore, a kind of mortar which binds the separate units of experience together. It is a serious matter, not a trivial one, to give up the observance of these festivals in a home, in a church, in the state. In so doing we break faith with ourselves, with our most intimate personal memories and our longer social hopes. We are more lonely thereafter, more cut off from those we love and those with whom we do the day's work.

The next thing to be said about Christmas is that it stands for the priority of persons in our world. Years ago Phillips Brooks said of the first Christmas, "A father and a mother and a child are there. No religion which began like that could ever lose its character." The longer one lives the more one realizes that it is the persons in one's world who matter most. Some learn this too late. After Jane Carlyle's death Thomas Carlyle read over her private papers which were wet with his tears, as he said again and again, "If I had only known. If I had only known." One ought not to leave that knowledge too long and thus too late.

There is no other day in all the year when this conviction asserts itself so bravely, despite all the tawdry apparatus, as on Christmas Day. We try to think, first of all, of the persons who really matter to us and in turn are strengthened and reassured to find that there are others to whom apparently we matter. To know that and to live in that knowledge saves one from that most deadly of all our human maladies, the sense of loneliness in an empty world.

This brings us to the religious heart of the matter. In our own turn we may still be warranted, three hundred years and more after the days of Governor Bradford, in distrusting the almost ineradicable pagan strain in Christmas and to dissent from what may seem to be its theological errors. But the first syllable in that word, not the last, is the important one. Therefore, the day states again the old imperious question, "What think ye of Christ?" and thus, "What think ye of Christianity?"

For more than thirty-five years now, which is the whole lifetime of the younger generation and the mature working years of the older generation, these have not been easy questions to answer. In the fall of 1914 men were freely saying that the boys would be out of the trenches by Christmas. The Korean War also brought its inopportune hopes. Failure to redeem these hopes brings us up to Christmas not merely with a feeling of frustration but even of cynicism. Everyone who broods over the mystery of human life has been at times invaded by the sinister suggestion that keeping Christmas under such circumstances is a matter of sheer escapism or deliberate self-deception. This mood is, after all, nothing new. The mystics have always known it, and have a name for it. They call it The Dark Night of the Soul.

Even on this cynical basis the historic fact of Jesus is not denied. He can be conceded and admired and even followed afar off. He would still stand in the forefront of all that is meant by human progress. He had climbed higher up its tedious slopes than any other man. In Tennyson's words he had come to the point where the yelp of the beast had been silenced and where man can be quiet at last. But like every other kindred soul struggling painfully upward he had to cry at the last, "My God, my God, why hast thou forsaken me?"

Much if not most of our religion is, after all, a thing of self-discipline and earnest, honest moral strain. Matthew Arnold was wholly faithful to the tempers of Anglo-Saxon Protestantism when he said that life is three quarters conduct and that religion is morality touched with emotion. It is out of the repeated frustration of such a religion, which is human-all-too-human, that our sense of failure and our moods of both skepticism and cynicism come.

So it is that one comes back to the Christmas stories in the New Testament in years like these more aware than ever that the whole movement of their thought is in precisely the opposite direction. All the world was being taxed, taxed in more ways than one. There was no room for the child in the inn. All that he stood for seemed crowded out. The wise men came, but went away again into their own country, a far country. Superficially these things seem as true now as they were then. But in spite of all this there is no sense of strain in the Gospel record of Christmas, there is no fear of defeat, and there certainly is no cynicism. There is only a great serenity. The stories of the annunciation to Mary, the angel songs which the shepherds heard, the adoration of the Magi, the presentation in the Temple are quiet and tranquil. No matter whether one is a biblical Fundamentalist or a modernist, the record makes the same impression on all alike and we bow to it. At this point we know that "the Bible is true because it finds us." The story is not that of man struggling painfully onward and upward forever, only to be disillusioned at the last, but of God coming down to enter into and share our human life. The whole gospel narrative is woven around that one golden thread. It first appears in the poems of nativity. It is reaffirmed many years afterward in the reflective prologue to the Gospel of John. By the time that prologue was written Christians had already tasted the tribulation that is in the world. They had been burned as torches in Nero's gardens. Nevertheless, the light that lighteth every man went on shining in the darkness and the darkness had not been able to put it out. What was true then is still true. Nothing that history has done to man, or that men have done to one another in history, has ever put out that light.

Now all this is a matter of faith. It is not knowledge in the sense in which we use that word most accurately. "We have but faith: we cannot know, For knowledge is of things we see." For we are dealing here with the unseen eternal world. There died not long ago one of the most devout Christians in our Western World, Dr. Hensley Henson, one-time Bishop of Durham. He was by mental habit a man of critical temperament, even to the point of native skepticism. But at the end of his long life of single-minded concern for Christianity he said, "I am still often brought to a sharp halt by some new challenge to Christianity or by some uprush of old challenges which, though silenced for a while, have never been effectively banished. In these distressful crises I have often been rescued by the method of imagining that I have committed myself to the defence of the anti-Christian side. Then I have discovered that in spite of all its ragged edges and unsolved problems, Christianity seems to provide the stronger case. I would rather be charged with its advocacy than with that of its opposite. . . . There is nothing comparable to the continued influence of Jesus in the history of religion. The marks of Jesus are silently impressed on his true disciples in the normal procedure of society as well as in the crises of suffering and martyrdom."

May I venture to pass on my own feeling for Christmas in this troubled year. I no longer feel cynical at its return and its observance now, as I once felt. I no longer feel guilty of escapism or of willful self-deception and insincerity. That for which the day stands seems more real, more true, and morally more inevitable than it once seemed. Our world has been straying far, very far, at times, from the highway of our God and to our God. But many of the ways into which we have fallen are dead ends. Even in the order of nature they must frustrate and defeat themselves. The Kingdom of God may not come soon or cheaply on earth, as it is in heaven. But that it must come and in the providence of God will come in his time seems more and more certain.

One may say, This after all is what a parson and preacher is professionally paid to say. He must, as in duty bound, repeat once more these frayed platitudes. The striking thing about our times is not the professional rehearsal again of old theological conventions by ministers: it is their rediscovery by other unsubsidized men: soldiers, lawyers, and at least some statesmen as a firsthand conclusion and conviction.

Let me end with a single witness to this sober change going on slowly in many such minds. He is the most unlikely man in circles like our own to have said any such thing. For years he has flung his jibes at religion and still does not hesitate to criticize its contemporary forms; Bertrand Russell. He recently gave a series of lectures at Columbia on "The Impact of Science on Society." He began his lectures by saying that the philosophy of human power is a very dangerous one, and if unchecked may end in disastrous consequences. Then he ended the lectures with these words, "The root of the matter is a very simple old-fashioned thing, a thing so simple I am almost ashamed to mention it for fear of the derisive smile with which wise cynics will greet my words. The thing I mean —please forgive me for mentioning it—is love, Christian love, or compassion. If you feel this you have a motive for existence, a guide for action, a reason for courage, an imperative necessity for intellectual honesty."

XVI

EMOTION RECOLLECTED IN TRANQUILLITY

Text: The light shineth in darkness; and the darkness comprehended it not.—JOHN 1:5

A HUNDRED years ago most Christians believed that the Bible was an infallible book, verbally inspired by God. In the case of English-speaking Christians that Bible was our familiar King James version. This belief still survives in many of the more conservative churches and it is the occasion for most of the adverse criticism which is now being addressed to the latest translation of the Bible. Fundamentalists say that fallible men are not competent to alter an infallible text.

In the main the changes made in any modern retranslation of the Bible are not radical. They do not affect what may be called the substance of the faith. But here and there they do correct what was an actual mistranslation in the King James Bible. The text is a case in point. The old version says of the light that shines in the darkness that the darkness did not comprehend it. The verse makes good sense in those words. The light that came into the world was Christ and it is quite true to say that the world did not comprehend him, understand and accept him. The passage in which our text is found said very truly that he came unto his own and his own received him not. That is still true of many persons today. Emerson says that sensual persons cannot understand Jesus. He is an enigma, a meaningless figure to them. He is at best Swinburne's pale Galilean, at whose touch the world has grown cold. There is inherently nothing wrong with the statement that a world of darkened people cannot comprehend Jesus.

But that is not what the Fourth Gospel said or meant and at this point the modern translations are more faithful to the original. The Revised Standard Version says, "The light shines in the darkness, and the darkness has not overcome it." Dr. Goodspeed's still more vernacular version says, "The light is still shining in the darkness, for the darkness has never put it out."

That is the mystery and the miracle of the Christian religion. At almost every period of its history, and especially in our own time, skeptics and critics have prophesied the imminent collapse of Christianity. At the end of World War I it was widely said that Christianity could not hope to survive those years. It had not prevented the war in the first place, it had done little to ameliorate it, and after the war was over it stood discredited in the eyes of the world. There is far more warrant for such appraisal of the facts now, after World War

II, than there was then. There are, it is true, great nations, once nominally Christian, where its main ideas are disallowed and prohibited. Yet even there Christianity still survives in hidden catacombs. The end is not yet. And in our own imperfectly Christian world our religion is far from being dead and gone. Improbable and unexpected persons keep telling us that only in the Christian doctrines of faith and hope and love can we find confidence for the future. "Lord, to whom shall we go? thou hast the words of eternal life."

Someone said the other day that it seemed to him that the Christmas season through which we have just passed has been a little less raucous, a little less blatant than any of its predecessors in past years, a little more sensitive in its observance. One is not sure that he is not right. Lincoln said that in the crises of the Civil War he was driven to his knees because he had nowhere else to go. President Truman has bidden us to pray for our world and in particular for our enemies, not for our own sake merely but their sake as well. These are not the words of the run-of-the-mill politician, nor are they common words with even the greatest statesmen. Yet something in us acknowledges their timeless truth.

I once received a Christmas card with a photograph of a great stone arch, perhaps a hundred feet high, standing in one of the more remote areas of our southwestern desert. It was obviously carved out untold centuries ago by running water and by wind-driven sand. It survived because it was harder stuff than the stratum of which it was once a part.

Let me come at our idea by way of a half dozen lines from one of John Masefield's sonnets:

These myriad days, these many thousand hours,
A man's long life, so choked with dusty things,
How little perfect poise with perfect powers,
Joy at the heart and beauty at the springs,
One hour, or two, or three, in long years scattered
Are all that life has given and all that mattered.[1]

Masefield tends to be a rather melancholy man. Not all of us think as badly of life as he does. Much of life seems and indeed is transient. But some of it survives because of an enduring worth of its own. And yet we can all understand what he meant. For a vast amount of life apparently has to be devoted to chores which do not appear to have in them the enduring stuff of anything like their own inherent eternal life. One of the most devoted English scholars of the last generation, Canon Sanday of Christ Church in Oxford, once told his class that three quarters of the honest intellectual work of the world is sheer mental drudgery. And our own President Eliot was quoted as having said that nine tenths of his work had to be unashamed academic drudgery.

Again the ratio may seem too hard and too high, yet once again we know what the poet and the scholar and the administrator meant. Living a life and making a character are processes which require a great deal of scaffolding outside the interior building. Over most of the process the scaffolding conceals what is going on within; that amount of scaffolding is necessary, but it is temporary. It is not meant to last. Well, so it is with the day's work. We do not ask permanence for the scaffolding of life's drudgery. We only know that without it there could never be the finished work within.

---

[1] From *Good Friday and Other Poems*. Used by permission of The Macmillan Company.

William Wordsworth, in his description of the poet's experience, once coined a far-reaching phrase about "emotion recollected in tranquillity." He had in mind not so much the remembrance of past emotions as their reanimation—the actual living of them over again as present feelings. The most important of our experiences always involve the emotions. But at any given moment it is hard to distinguish between shallow feelings which are sentimental and deeper feelings which foster true emotions. Not only so, but all of us have had the experience of being unable to grasp at the moment of their happening the meaning of the really important events in our lives. It may be a wise provision of Nature or Providence that this is so. Those moments or hours or days are best understood in anticipation and in memory. More, even, in memory than in anticipation. For only memory can appeal to emotion recollected in tranquillity. There is no one of us who does not bear in his mind and heart the scars of past pain and sorrow and sin. But somehow the feelings which once accompanied them do not have the enduring quality which lives on in our memories of life's good and happy experiences. That very fact should reassure us that life and the world are meant to be and in the main are good rather than evil. In any case, "emotion recollected in tranquillity" is one of the best ways to measure the depth of our experiences.

We read as our second lesson the majestic prologue to St. John's Gospel. That Gospel was written perhaps a hundred years after the birth of Jesus. The stories of the Nativity of Christ to which we have listened again during the last few days are utterly lovely. But in our hard-bitten and realistic world we are sometimes tempted, as they recur, to think of them as perhaps rather sentimental. They are for us, and probably were meant to be from the first, poetry rather than factual prose. But the prologue to St. John's Gospel is also one of the Nativity stories, only that it is emotion recollected in tranquillity. It recovers not merely the religious truth of the tales of the birth of Christ, but more than that. As it stands in the Gospels it affirms the depth and genuineness and importance of the whole experience of Jesus had by the first disciples and by the two generations which had intervened before the latest of the Gospels was written. All of St. John's Gospel is, in fact, the record recollected in tranquillity of the emotions which Christians had attached and still attach to their discipleship to Christ.

For those of us who in any way dare to call ourselves Christians the opening verses of John are a perpetual witness to the truth and worth of our experience of discipleship to Christ. One cannot read those great words unmoved; our own deepest experiences of life still go back to them. They reassure us that what we call "the mind of Christ" was and is a transcript of the first and final truth of things. They persuade us that however irrational and unideal the life of the moment may seem, there is hidden behind the mystery of things what Wordsworth himself once called an "Eternity of Thought," for that is what the term "Word" means, and that this Eternity of Thought has come and tabernacled with us in Christ Jesus our Lord. He was not and is not, for us, what the biologists call a "sport" in the order of nature and history. He is their passkey and their truth. However seldom we use that passkey and however poorly we grasp that truth, it is still true that heaven and earth shall pass away, but his words have not passed away. For the purposes of our daily life the emotions which prompt and attend that belief can always be recollected in tranquillity. We simply cannot warm up and warm over the ephemeral sentimental feelings of many of these past years. They had no promise of endurance as we recover them in memory. But anyone with any feeling for the Christian religion will never fail to find that his past experience of his religion will always be an emotion that can be recollected in tranquillity.

This Sunday after Christmas and before the New Year is an equivocal day. The formal Christian calendar makes no allowance for New Year's Day. That day is the survival of a pagan festival celebrating the rebirth of the Unconquered Sun. In its own way it is the festival of light reasserting itself in the darkness. None of us is entirely indifferent to the birth of another year. "Who can think," said Meredith, "and not think hopefully?" Who can put the old calendar away and turn to a new one without "thinking hopefully"? If it be true that the three greatest things in the world are faith and hope and love, our Christian hope is not for anything like absolute novelty, for in the realm of religion there is little novelty. But we can turn with good confidence to another year bringing with us the Christian emotions which we recollect in tranquillity. The light is still shining in the darkness and the darkness has not been able to put it out.

XVII

THE OLD AND NEW YEARS

Text: We are troubled on every side, yet not distressed; we are perplexed, but not in despair.—II CORINTHIANS 4:8

H IS first disciples believed that Jesus would return to earth during their lifetime to rule over the finally realized Kingdom of God. The earliest books in the New Testament, St. Paul's Epistles to the Thessalonians, are mainly concerned with this expectation. St. Paul tells his converts in Thessalonica what the second coming will be like, what will happen to them when that time comes, how they are to occupy themselves until Christ comes and what is to be done for those who have died in the meantime. They are not to be idle or careless about everyday life. They are to keep on with their work.

How far Jesus himself was responsible for this belief is one of the most difficult problems in the whole history of Christian thought. Did Jesus tell his disciples that this was what was going to happen? There are in the first three Gospels many sayings which suggest that he believed that the end of the present world order was at hand, that the Kingdom of God was imminent and that he himself would come back to reign over it.

If he said those words did he mean them in a literal sense or were they spoken as spiritual parables? Or, again, were they wished back on Jesus by disciples and writers who held such ideas quite independent of him and thus imputed them to him, as many of us do to this day when we read the Gospels?

Be these things as they may, before the first century had ended and the New Testament was in the main concluded, the first Christians had given up the premature hope that Christ would come back in their own lifetime. The Gospel of John, which was written around the year 100, has nothing to say about Jesus' speedy second coming. In the place of that doctrine we find instead the doctrine of the Comforter, the Holy Spirit of Christ which is to be with us always, which is to call Christ to our remembrance and continue, in his name, to guide and teach us. With this doctrine Christian history unfolded before the Church, stretching away into an indeterminate future, to which it could see no clearly dated end.

There have always been and still are some literal Second Adventists in Christian circles. They have increased in numbers during the last few years because the history of our times has persuaded many devout people that these years must be marking the end of the present world order, since the world cannot go on much longer in the way in which it has been going. But in the main the Christian Church has cast its lot with the doctrine of the Holy Spirit which is found in John's Gospel. Modern Christians for the most part do not expect to see Jesus coming back in his earthly form to take over the rule of the world.

Century after century the Christian Church has had to accommodate itself to new knowledge unknown to its founders. In so doing it has often seemed to compromise its faith and to lose its sacred heritage. But somehow it has not merely known the pain of these acts of intellectual accommodation; it has survived them and kept something of its own distinctive quality. Theologically, the Christianity which we profess today is not, literally, the religion of Jesus. Nevertheless, the spirit of the Beatitudes survives and we believe their simple words.

It has often seemed to me that of all the painful readjustments which Christians have had to make in the letter of their faith that which was required of them toward the end of the first century must have been the most painful. They had been brought up to believe in the immediate second coming of Christ. They had to reckon with the fact that he had not yet come and that perhaps he would not come in the form which they had expected. The wonder is that they did not lose their faith and give up their religion. The marvel is that the Christian religion itself ever negotiated that high pass between the first books of the New Testament and the second century which unrolled before it, like a great plain, stretching away for what must have seemed to be endless years to come. If it be true that hope deferred maketh the heart sick, then the pain and sickness which our religion must have suffered in this way so long ago might well have been fatal.

We are told today that Christianity is dying before our eyes, that what is called our loss of religion must be accepted as an all but achieved fact. Let us grant that it has not been easy for the Christians of the last hundred years to make a place for new knowledge within the historic framework of their faith. That knowledge proves to be progressively great and in its own right must prevail. A Christianity which tries to deny it or obstruct it is fighting a losing battle, although it still remains a fair question whether any of this knowledge nullifies, for example, the Beatitudes or Paul's chapter on charity.

My own conviction is that in so far as there is any such loss of Christianity going on in our times it is due mainly to a creeping suspicion that, lovely as the Christian ethic may be, it is impracticable, so much so as to be now incredible. A famous Lutheran pastor named Naumann during World War I said, when he gave up his concern for Christianity and cast his lot with the secular state, that Christianity hangs like high white clouds of longing over our hard factual world.

This is the more true of American Protestantism, because our hopes by the end of the nineteenth century were set very high. The social gospel was making tremendous headway. It looked as though the Holy Commonwealth which our forefathers had come here to found was not too far away. Ancient abuses were being corrected. Hoary and stubborn evils in society were being cast out. Our expectation was of a much speedier advent of the Kingdom of God than we had supposed. We were not merely morally optimistic; we were ethically impetuous. We were too self-confident to bother any longer to read the parable of Jesus spoken to those who mistakenly believed that the Kingdom of Heaven was just at hand. With the best will in the world they were proved wrong. One remembers the remark made by Miss Comstock when she left the presidency of Radcliffe College. She said that upon looking back she realized that she had made one serious mistake; she had underestimated the positiveness of evil.

In any case, in this mid-twentieth century we find ourselves back in the position of the Christians of the first century who had to adjust their minds to the fact that Christ was not coming back to earth in their lifetime. All of us today are having to adjust our minds to the hard fact that what we mean by the Kingdom of God is not as near as we had once hoped and believed. Many of us are by habit going on with the outward observance of our religion, but in the back of our minds there is the gnawing suspicion that we may be merely the dauntless soldiers of a forlorn hope. The problem is whether, in our time, we can make the sort of transition which those first Christians made so long ago.

There is no doubt that St. Paul himself made this radical readjustment in his own thinking. His last epistles no longer elaborate the expectation which prompted his first epistles. When he remade his mind, and how and why we cannot say. When I was doing theology in Oxford I was taught that it was probably made between the First and the Second Epistles to the Corinthians. The two letters are very different in their texture and spirit. Something had happened to the man in the meantime. It may have been illness, it may have been suffering for his cause, it may have been attacks from his enemies. In any case he was not in the Second Epistle the same man who had written the First Epistle. One can only say that the

man who wrote the Second Epistle was not merely a more
sober man, more of a realist, but a more mature man than the
man who wrote the First Epistle.

We might recall the great chapter in the First Epistle on
charity—on love. I am not certain that II Corinthians 4 is
not a still greater bit of Christian writing. However that may
be, the fourth chapter of II Corinthians is certainly more
timely today in that it is a more faithful transcript of our
own situation.

We are coming to the end of another of these difficult and
equivocal years through which it has been our lot to live. If
one goes to political and economic newsmen, who are supposed
to be standing in the watch towers of the world, and asks,
"Watchman, what of the night?" one will get the same reply
that the prophet Isaiah got centuries ago: "The morning
cometh, and also the night: if ye will inquire, inquire ye:
return, come." There seem to be some signs of the dawning
of a brighter day, but that dawn is not yet assured. It is still
nighttime. Come back again and ask once more. That is all
that the forecaster can tell you. Therefore, with St. Paul we
are turned back from the uncertain and as yet unsettled events
in the world around us to our own frame of mind.

In the years between the wars the distinguished editor of
the *Atlantic Monthly,* Mr. Ellery Sedgwick, said of our
personal political opinions, "We are not going to stand still
and stay as we are. We shall become either more conservative
or more radical." Something of the same sort must be said of
our religion. It will not remain the rather conventional thing
it has been. Either we shall slowly give it up altogether or

else we shall become more persuaded of its truth. One might ask oneself, "Am I at the end of this year more religious or less religious than I was at its beginning. Which way are my mind and my heart moving?"

I can only commend to you St. Paul's meditations upon his own experience. To begin with, he had realized that human nature is not as unbreakable as he had once supposed. He saw this in the world around him and he probably realized it in himself. There is a wealth of personal experience behind that line, "We have this treasure in earthen vessels." It is, in its way, one of the truest and yet most poignant sentences in the whole Bible. The person who does not know what it means is hardly fitted to face the future and serve his generation. The broken vessels of our fragile humanity lie all over the face of the earth. And in his own life no one has reason to be overconfident of the earthen container of whatever precious spirit he may personally profess to have.

St. Paul then goes on to describe his actual situation. He is entirely free of any romantic sentimentality. The words are coldly prose and realistic. He was "troubled on every side." He was "perplexed, and persecuted and cast down." Very few of us here have been actually persecuted, although persecution of Christians, because of their Christianity, has become today a tragic commonplace—as much so as in the days of the lions and the gladiators in the time of the Roman arena. But all of us have been troubled, sometimes cast down, and most of all we have been constantly perplexed. What is the effect of these troubles and depressions and perplexities to be upon our own inner life?

Well, I can only recommend to you St. Paul's own second thoughts. He was not distressed, he was not in despair, he was not forsaken, he was not destroyed.

If we could take our farewell of the old year and face the new year with this realism on the one hand and this untroubled serenity on the other hand, we could look back on the one without bitterness and look forward to the other without panic or despair. Many of the things which we have been seeing and may yet see are temporal, intensely and indubitably so. But there are also the unseen things of which St. Paul so confidently speaks and they are eternal.

XVIII

THE TRIBULATION THAT IS IN THE WORLD
A Sermon for Palm Sunday

Text: In the world ye shall have tribulation: but be of good cheer; I have overcome the world.—JOHN 16:33

SOME time ago one of the more Protestant members of this congregation stood looking at that table down on the platform between this pulpit and the lectern. He seemed afraid that it was an altar in disguise. Finally he said, "If you ever put a cross on that table I shall never come in here again." What made him feel that way? What made him say that?

He was a man who stood in the old Puritan tradition. He was by heritage and mental habit very anti-Catholic. He probably thought of the cross as being primarily, if not solely, a Roman symbol and as a Protestant of the older type he was still in revolt against any survival of Catholicism.

Once again, though he was culturally an eighteenth-century Puritan he was theologically very liberal. Like many such persons he probably did not wish to seem to commit himself to

147

any of the now almost incredible doctrines of atonement
which have been identified with the cross. The theory that
God placated his anger against sinful humanity by accepting
the death of his son on the cross as a vicarious offering of
penitence no longer accords with our thought of God nor our
understanding of an ethical world.

Finally, it may well be that the man in question was not
unique, but was simply one of ourselves, a natural human
being who shrank from the whole idea of suffering in which
the cross is rooted, and from which we instinctively turn
away. He was not to be blamed for that reaction, nor are we
to be blamed if we share it with him.

The Holy Week story, from Palm Sunday on through Good
Friday to Easter, is to most of us more than familiar. Unlike
many tragedies which we see or which we read, it has no
novelty for us. The observance of Holy Week asks of us what
is always one of the hardest acts to which the mind can ad-
dress itself, the reanimation of a truth that is in perennial danger of becoming a lifeless platitude. Coleridge says that the
only way to do that is to ponder the truth with direct reference to oneself and one's own life.

Let us, then, take as our point of departure for the moment
those words of the Christ in St. John's gospel, "In the world
ye shall have tribulation." This is not the first time that the
Bible commits itself to this fact of life. You remember the old
verse in Job, "Man is born unto trouble, as the sparks fly
upward." It takes a deliberate act of mental and moral recollection for us to turn and face and accept those words,
whether in Job or in John.

In particular, ideas of trouble and tribulation as being a constant and perhaps a necessary part of our experience have been rather alien to the American temperament, and indeed to its religion. The most accurate description of the Christian religion which I know, and it is a description not a definition, is that of Father Tyrrell, "Christianity is an ultimate optimism, founded upon a provisional pessimism." American Protestantism has tended to evade the provisional pessimism. Much of the old orthodoxy preserved and professed the most melancholy views of human nature and our human lot, but over all our history we have been a hopeful people, and the pursuit of happiness rather than the cultivation of trouble has been our native concern. The pessimist has been out of step with our American culture. Thus, John Ruskin once wrote to Charles Eliot Norton that he did not care to visit America because he doubted whether he could stand what he called its spirit of "over-hopefulness and getting-on-ness."

If those of us who have lived through this last half century were asked, "What is the most important date in your life?" I think most of us would reply, "August 4, 1914, the day when World War I began." It was then, so to speak, that the iceberg began to roll over under our feet. It has not really found its new center of gravity yet. And for nearly forty years we have lived in a world where as a generation we have had tribulation.

There are three ways of trying to deal with the tribulation that is in the world, its moral troubles, its mental and emotional troubles, its physical troubles. The first way is to deny that there is any trouble, that what we think of as trouble has no reality or existence. This method is very ancient as well as modern. What is more, up to a point, it will work and work well. It certainly is well to apply it to all of life's lesser troubles.

The next method is to fight it, head on. Thus Mr. Wells said of his Invisible King that he would have to die on a cross, but that in dying he would wrench one hand free from the nail and shake his fist in the face of the Veiled Being who determines the course of human life.

The third way is to accept candidly and without savage resentment the tribulation that is in the world and then try to change its signs from negative to positive. It takes a good deal of experience of life and no little discipline by life to come to this frame of mind, but most of us do come to it or at least toward it.

If the truth be told all of us learn from our own moral failures and sins lessons that could hardly be learned in any other way. In the end, if we accept the discipline of hard moral experience, our characters, and with them, our human sympathies are more mature than otherwise they could have been. This being so, there is, as St. Paul knew, the subtle temptation to sin merely that grace may abound, and that, as Paul said, we may not and must not do. The pleasure of the sin is too often condoned by the prospective luxury of repentance.

Well, so also, of these nearly forty years of the world's tribulation. Our little personal troubles are all set within the circle of the world's great troubles. But the danger of the moment is that we develop a perverse taste for trouble. We accept the unhappy endings of our plays and novels with an unhealthy consent. And in religion, the love of normal life and the pursuit of it seem defeated by these prolonged years of the world's tribulation.

We do not get from our religion, or from its source in the teaching of Jesus, specific answers to most of the pressing practical problems which we face. But what we do get from the Gospels is the strong conviction that in the terms of his own life and mission Jesus was no stranger to such issues. What we get from Jesus is the sense of comradeship, rather than the subject matter of advice. Thoreau once said, "A friend never descends to particulars, he advises by his whole behaviour." That is supremely true of Jesus. He advises us by his whole behaviour—and never more so than during the last week of his life when he faced and accepted the tribulation that is in the world. The record of Holy Week gives us more help than we can get from any theological or ethical system. Even to this day and at this day we may feel, in Masefield's words, "companioned still not left behind."

We ought not to allow our assurance of what may be called the "happy ending" of Holy Week in the Easter story to lessen in any way our feeling for the tribulation of the week itself. Paul himself was aware of our human tendency to strike straight for life's happy endings. He prays that we may know Christ and the power of his resurrection. Then he seems suddenly to realize that he is forgetting the days which preceded Easter and he revises his statement, to read, "That I may know him, and the power of his resurrection, and the fellowship of his sufferings."

We look forward to the time when we shall be reasonably

assured of a world at decent peace. Such a world, if and when it comes, will be a better world than any we have known hitherto. But we shall never see that world if we evade the fellowship of the sufferings of these days. We may feel, not without good reason, that it is little short of a cursed spite that we have been born to set the world aright. But if we ponder our lot again we may come to feel that if life has been a matter of living with tribulation in these years, such a life and lot may also be an honor conferred on us as a generation.

Remember the story in the Gospels of Simon of Cyrene. He was a Jew from Africa, coming up to Jerusalem to keep the feast. On the final stage of his journey he was stopped by a guard of the Roman army, impressed into their service, and made to carry the cross of a condemned criminal to the place of execution. All that he saw and shared in seems to have been the occasion for his becoming a Christian. Our generation, if you will, has been stopped as it was going about its lawful business and drafted to carry a burden of world-wide tribulation for which no one of us was responsible. The story has in it the passkey to the riddle of trouble. We cannot evade trouble, either, in our own private lives and we cannot fight it off. But if we accept it then we may overcome it, and it will be a source of a peace which otherwise we should never have attained. The tragedy of trouble is not the fact of suffering itself, but its wrong or ineffective use.

All this is a matter of what goes on in our meditative moments, of our maturing attitudes toward the tribulation that is in the world. The natural man strikes straight for the pleasures of life, its legitimate happiness. The Christian religion seems to intend to teach us that we cannot strike straight for those ends, we have to go the long way round of the tribulation that is in the world, and, as it were, earn the moral right to the happy ending.

I am minded to end these reflections with a quotation, a story, a much longer story perhaps than the best rules allow for a quotation. It is a tale heard by an English art critic, Robert Ross, and found in a recent book about him. No one seems to know its origin. The tale gives the two great contrasted views of life and the world; the pagan and the Christian. Robert Ross writes:

". . . I will, therefore, venture to relate a little story I heard in France some years ago, and never, I think, published. . . . I will not attempt to reproduce the French or the beautiful style of the original narrator.

"On a headland, overhanging the sea, which lies at the root of Mount Etna, there is a little shrine of a miraculous Madonna—the Madonna Stella Maris. She is the patron saint of the sailors, who bring her offerings from distant countries, and her festa is held on Midsummer Day. Mass on that day is always said before dawn, and then the chapel doors being carefully locked, are not opened until after sunset, when there is a Benediction, and a solemn procession at night with lighted torches. Hundreds of years ago, when St. Paul came to Syracuse, there was an image in this very shrine to the Cnidian Aphrodite, carved by some Greek sculptors, and brought by Greeks to Sicily. Her image could be seen far out at sea, through the pillars of the peristyle. Her face was turned to the east, and on Midsummer Day, at dawn, a ray of sun touched the lips of the goddess and she came down from her altar and talked to the priests, and told them those things which it is only lawful for priests to know. When the Emperor Constantine ruled in Rome priests of the new faith came and bricked up the open portico so that the sun could not touch the altar at any time, and they purified the shrine and sanctified it, and took away the image of the goddess, men said, to hack her to pieces. And after many years Christian priests put into the old shrine the figure of Our Lady. Her face was painted with harsh colours, such as those with which Sicilians still paint their gay wagons; but her face was sad, and full of pity. On her head was a gold Gothic crown, studded with gems, and on her hands were many wonderful rings. The cope was fastened over her breast with a brooch, shaped like a heart, in which there were seven swords. And she wrought many miracles, and even stayed a stream of lava from overwhelming the neighbouring town. Many princes and princesses passing through Sicily sent her rich gifts. Now, the priest who served the shrine saw one day that some of the bricks in the porch were loosened, for there had been an earthquake on the island. Fearing they might fall on some of the faithful he pulled them out and laid them on the marble steps. At dawn next morning a ray of light from the sun pierced into the dark shrine and touched the image on the lips. For it was Midsummer Day. And the wonder-working image came to life. And the sadness on her face was turned to joy. She smiled, as she stepped down from the altar and opened the chapel doors with a touch of her hands.

Down a pathway to the sea she walked, and found a little
pool of clear water in a cave, by the tideless sea. When she
saw her reflection she laughed, and washed away the Gothic
paint from her face, and took off the stiff cope from her body,
and the gold crown from her head, and the glittering rings
from her fingers, and hid them beneath a rock. She turned
to the sea and saw it was full of dolphins, and tritons, mermen
and mermaids. And on the yellow sands of the cave she saw
a little winged boy with bow and arrow. She cried to him
and he flew to her, and she knew that it was her son Eros.
And Eros asked his mother why she had been hiding; then
she smiled, and said, 'I will tell you before it is evening.' And
they went up from the sea coast into the glens of Etna.
Flowers that had died in the early summer heat bloomed
again, and the fauns came out of the woods, and the satyrs
called to each other, and the hamadryads and the nymphs
danced with them. . . . And Pan and the shepherds gambolled
as in the days of King Ptolemy Philadelphus because Eros and
Aphrodite were come to Sicily again. But when the mountains became purple, and the sun began to sink behind the
Pillars of Hercules, the face of Aphrodite was shadowed and
sad. She said farewell to the false Greek gods, and went
down to the sea with her son Eros, heavy at heart. And she
painted her face again with juices of flowers gathered by
Eros, and put on her head the tawdry gold crown and on her
fingers the glittering rings, and she clothed herself in the
stiff Byzantine robe, clasped with a heart and seven swords.
Slowly and sadly as the sun was sinking, she walked with
Eros to the shrine on the headland. Then Eros seemed to

know at last that she would leave him too, and he cried, 'Dear mother, why will you leave even me; and why will you go back to that dark sunless house of the strange God in a strange uncouth garment?' And Aphrodite bent down and kissed him; tears fell on her son's golden hair, and she said: 'Because I have yet another son, who has suffered greatly.' "[1]

---

[1] Margery Ross, *Robert Ross: Friend of Friends*. Published 1952, and used by permission of Jonathan Cape, Ltd. and Clarke, Irwin & Company, Ltd.

XIX

THE FELLOWSHIP OF HIS SUFFERINGS
A Sermon for Holy Week

Text: Then Pilate entered into the judgment hall again, and called Jesus, and said unto him, "Art thou the King of the Jews?" ... Jesus answered, "My kingdom is not of this world"
—JOHN 18:33-36

ST. AUGUSTINE tells us in his *Confessions* that as a young man he loved to go to the theater and see the Classic Greek tragedies. Looking back on his youth, as an older man, he asks, "Why is it that man likes thus to taste an unnecessary sorrow, by beholding distressing and tragical events which he would not wish to happen to himself? And yet as a spectator he wills to be touched with sorrow for them, and this sorrow is his pleasure."

The ancient world had its own answer to this question. The theater, particularly its tragedies, purges our emotions. Vague and deep feelings which have been repressed, or which at least have found no adequate outlet, are thus released.

Our frustrated emotions are voiced and played out for us on the stage. All of us have had this experience. Yet the fact remains, as St. Augustine says, that while as spectators we are touched with sorrow for them, we would not wish the distressing and tragic events which we behold to happen to ourselves. Hence, the solution of what may have been at first an emotional problem raises a far more serious moral problem. One of the medieval mystics, John Tauler, put the moral problem in a very bold figure. He said, "It shall be counted to a man as spiritual unchastity" to excite the deep emotions which we identify with religion, merely for the sake of the pleasure he gets in so doing.

The return of Holy Week always brings with it this moral peril. There is no other single narrative in our tradition as moving as the record of the last days in the life of Christ. This is particularly true of the accounts of the Last Supper, the Garden of Gethsemane, the arrest, the trials before the Sanhedrim and then before Pilate, the Via Dolorosa which led to Calvary, the crucifixion, the seven last words from the cross, and finally the descent from the cross and the entombment. We know these stories so well that they may have lost some of their freshness, yet no one can come seriously back to the observance of these days without still being moved by what he reads and hears and ponders in his heart. Rather than reread the record and remain unmoved, it might be better to give up altogether any attempt at its observance.

The gospel says of the ascent from Galilee to Jerusalem that Jesus went before his disciples. St. John says that, as the end drew near, Peter followed Jesus "afar off." That perhaps is the first impression which we get from the record. In the events as they unfold we are aware that Jesus goes before us, a long way before us, beyond anything we have ever experienced. He seems, as it were, to be so far ahead of us that we can hardly see him. What was true of Simon Peter is far more true of us; at best we follow afar off. We may not feel unfitted to have sat with the multitude on the hillside as he spoke the sermon on the mount. But to profess to have shared his passion is another matter. One is aware of what Nietzsche called "the pathos of distance" between ourselves and him. Sincerity requires that we do not claim too much for ourselves; that we admit from how far off we follow him.

Yet the strange thing is that both the Gospels and the subsequent New Testament do invite us to share the fellowship of the sufferings of Christ. We are not merely to try to follow him; we are to take up our own cross in the following. What is more, there is nothing in this invitation that is in any way alien to the mind and heart of Christ. He would wish it so. There are among our contemporaries, as Bishop Oxnam has recently told us, many heroes of the faith who in these days have followed Christ close at hand, rather than afar off. But just as the bishop asked himself and us whether we could have stood up to our times, could have followed them so closely and shared their experiences so fully, so we ask with even greater warrant when we try to keep Holy Week.

Nevertheless, as I have just suggested, there is in the New Testament this amazing generosity and catholicity, which does not shut out any of our little troubles from the fellowship of the sufferings of Christ. All of us must feel the discrep-

ancy between our share of the tribulation that is in the world
and the classic tribulation of Holy Week. It seems an impertinence to intrude our trivial crosses into the situation. Yet that
is just what Christianity dares us to do. No one of us ever lives
a life which does not know to some degree his part in the
tribulation that is in the world. The attempt to dodge or
shirk this fact is an evasion of life itself. We are perplexed
in mind, we suffer pains of the body, we are often defeated
and discouraged, we taste sorrow. And all these experiences
happen to us along what Thomas à Kempis calls the King's
Way of the Holy Cross. "Thou canst not escape it, whitherso-
ever thou runnest; for go where thou wilt thou carriest thyself
with thee; and shalt ever find thyself. Turn thyself upwards,
turn thyself downwards; turn thyself outwards, turn thyself
inwards; everywhere thou shalt find the Cross."

Matthew Arnold said of Shakespeare:

> All pains the immortal spirit must endure. . . .
> Find their sole speech in that victorious brow.

The same ascription, with far greater warrant, may be made
of Christ. There is no system of weights and measures by
which to distinguish between the various tribulations that
are in the world. If we can speak of greater or less, grave or
trivial, they are still all of a kind. And that is why there is
no incongruity in daring to accept the great generosity of the
Christian invitation to share the fellowship of Christ's sufferings. All pains our spirit must endure are entitled to be brought
to Calvary and laid there, if we come with sincerity and
good conscience.

If Christianity does not encourage us to deny or evade these pains, this tribulation that is in the world, it does offer to give us good cheer and help us to overcome the world, rather than to lapse into despair and be defeated by the world. One of the most profound sermons preached during the last century is that by James Martineau on "Great Principles and Small Duties." He says that we too often think that it is beneath the dignity of a great principle to apply it to some small duty. A small principle should suffice for a small duty. Whereas, the truth is that only a great principle is sufficient to inspire and sustain us in life's small duties.

Something of precisely this same sort is true of the Christian reference of what may seem our small troubles to the great tribulation which we meet as the Gospels move on through Holy Week. None of us is likely to be martyred this week. None of us is likely to be doomed to a painful persecution. None of us is going to be suddenly and totally impoverished. Our lives will go on. But none of us is wholly quit of what may seem to be his all but negligible and trivial share in the world's tribulations. The ability to meet and bear and overcome any of these only too familiar tribulations of everyday life must derive from a great principle. And the secret of victory over that tribulation is written somewhere into the record of the days between Palm Sunday and Easter. Indeed, the secret of Christianity, of all religion, had begun to be written into the story at the very beginning of the Gospels, where another realm of things seems to come down and share in the life of our imperfect world.

It has been said that religion is the attempt to live in two worlds at the same time. One of these worlds is our actual here and now world which we know only too well. The other of these worlds is a different world. If one is thinking of ethics and morality it will be called an ideal world. If one is thinking of religion it must be called the real world. The difference between an ideal world and a real world is this: the former is the far-off future goal of our moral struggle; the latter is in existence even now and I suppose one must say that it has its reality in the mind of God and thus in Godlike persons here and now. The actual and the real worlds seldom coincide. There is in all religion a contrast and tension between them. It is relatively easy to resign from the actual world and try to live only in the real world. It is still easier to give up all attempt to live in the real world and make the best one can of the actual world. But if one does either of these things one loses what is the quality of all religion, this attempt to live in two worlds at the same time. It is the moral discrepancy between the ways of the two worlds which troubles us most. One might say that to be aware of that discrepancy is, thus far, to be religious. Indeed a parson broadcasting in Canada did say it not long ago, "An uneasy conscience makes a better Christian than a sense of complacency." So, the Gospel says of Christ's disciples that they should be in the world, but not of the world.

The basic religious difficulty of our times rises from the fact that preoccupation with this present actual world is crowding out of our minds and hearts our awareness of the real world. In so far as we are Christians we must believe—even if this be an act of faith—that the Realm of God is a real world, the most real of all worlds. It is neglect and forget-fulness of this conviction—not so much denied as crowded out by imperative concerns in our actual world—that is the source of what is called our present-day loss of religion.

Whatever else Holy Week may mean to us in this troubled and difficult year, it is a summons to us to try to understand and enter, as far as we can do so, into the words of our text, "My kingdom is not of this world."

XX

LIFE ETERNAL
An Easter Sermon

Text: Father, into thy hands I commend my spirit.—Luke 23:46

LIFE and the world are forever putting questions to us. Some of these questions are practical and urgent and must be answered at once. Others are theoretical and may be put off indefinitely. Yet these latter are on the whole the more important. The difficulty is that the answers have to be matters of faith rather than of knowledge, and we moderns are far too inclined to try to make knowledge do duty for faith.

Years ago a leader of the Ethical Culture Society in Boston announced in the Saturday papers that at the meeting of his Society on Easter Sunday morning he would discuss the soft coal strike in Kentucky. Somehow his choice of a subject seemed either an evasion of a moral duty or a great opportunity missed.

Easter Day is the classic Christian answer to the old stubborn question in the book of Job, "If a man die, shall he live again?" The Christian answer to the question has always been an unequivocal "Yes." Without that answer the Christian religion would never have come into being. And by that answer our religion has survived century after century. Nevertheless, the form of the answer itself proposes new problems of its own and Job's anxious query still persists.

On the whole it is to the moral credit of the modern world that we are not hagridden by this problem. Countless sincere persons are willing to leave the question unanswered in an earnest endeavor to make this earth a little more like what a heaven ought to be. In the course of the first crusade King Louis met in Palestine an old Saracen woman carrying a torch in one hand and a jug of water in the other hand. When she was asked by the king what she was doing with these, she replied that she was going to put out the fires of hell and burn up the joys of heaven that men might love God for his own sake. She was seeking what the medieval mystics used to call the unmercenary love of God, and what a modern author has called the high religion of dispassionateness. There is, in this secular rather than theological form, a great deal of that temper abroad among serious persons in our time.

Meanwhile, Dean Inge once said that God cannot be very real to persons who think of him only about two minutes in the day. So, we might say that an after-life cannot be very real, or even very important to those who think of it only once a year at Eastertide. Yet there are times when Job's question reasserts itself. It confronts us when there is someone near and dear to us whom we have loved and lost. Is the beloved lost, as Newman's hymn says, only "awhile," or is the beloved lost finally and forever? One cannot look thoughtfully at those names on the south wall of Memorial Church, the men of Harvard who died in World War II, or the names of their predecessors in the earlier memorial room beyond, without being aware of Job's question, which for the most part lies dormant in the back of the mind. Are those thousand men perished as though they had never been? Is there nothing left of them save in our remembrance? It may be hard to imagine how and where they are living a still ongoing life. But it somehow seems a premature, presumptuous and ungenerous act to say that there is for them no such life.

The truth is that faith in some life other than this, after and beyond this, is not, as is so often charged, primarily a selfish affair. Mr. H. G. Wells in an unusual moment of self-disparagement once said that he would not want a God who could afford to be bothered with him eternally. One has the feeling that Mr. Wells would be very annoyed with a God who was not bothered with him.

It is by no means impossible to contemplate for oneself something like total annihilation. We are, for example, a tired generation, and we can understand that touching epitaph in the old German cemetery at Lubec, "When thou callest me, Lord Christ, I will arise, but first let me rest awhile for I am very weary." We can even go on and be prepared to accept, if need be, those lines written by his wife which Huxley asked to have cut into his tombstone:

> For so he giveth his beloved sleep,
> And if an endless sleep he wills, so best.

What concerns most of us in this mysterious matter is not

so much our own destiny, as the destiny of those whom we have loved and lost, the destiny of those who in the service of great causes have laid down their life on earth when it was hardly begun, indeed the nature and destiny of humanity itself. The problem is not that of a self-centered you or me, but of mankind in its entirety.

Some years ago Henry Adams wrote a most pessimistic book about the *Degradation of the Democratic Dogma*. He based it upon the then accepted second law of thermodynamics which holds that our world is running down and that we are involved in this catastrophe. He gives pictoral point to his thought by a quotation from Camille Flammarion, a French astronomer. The passage runs as follows. As the world becomes colder,

Life and human activity will be shut up within the tropical zones. Saint Petersburg, Berlin, London, Paris, Vienna, Constantinople, Rome will sink to sleep under their eternal cerements. During many centuries, equatorial humanity will undertake vain arctic explorations to rediscover under the ice the sites of Paris, of Bordeaux, of Lyons, of Marseilles. No longer will man live, down to the day when the last tribe, already expiring of cold and hunger, shall camp in the rays of a pale sun which will henceforth illumine an earth that is only a wandering tomb. Soon their bones will be buried under the shroud of eternal ice. The historian of nature would then be able to write, "Here lies the entire humanity of a world which has lived. Here lie all the dreams of ambition, all the conquests of military glory, all the resounding affairs of finance, all the systems of an imperfect science, and also all the oaths of mortals' love. Here lie all the beauties of the earth." But no mortuary stone will mark the spot where the poor planet shall have rendered its last sigh.

Something of the sort may well be the terrestrial destiny of this planet. Our dust will then be embalmed in ice. But if there is no spirit that shall have returned to God who gave it, does it really make sense? It does not seem to me to make sense, unimaginable as the terms of any other destiny may be.

Our natural sciences discover in the remotest star the same elements which we know here. Iron is iron there as well as here. If there is in the total scheme of things some personal principle, it is very hard to believe that all our human thoughtfulness, with its idealisms and its affections, has no commerce or connection with that principle. It is hard not to share Browning's conviction, "O heart I made a heart beats here."

We seldom realize how deep this conviction is in the mind and heart of man, when men dare to trust their uncensored instincts and intuitions. This sense of identification with the whole of things is, in a very elemental form, written into Wordsworth's "Lines to Lucy":

> No motion has she now, no force,
>   She neither hears nor sees,
> Rolled round in earth's diurnal course
>   With rocks, and stones and trees.

So of the lines which Robert Louis Stevenson wrote as he was coming to the end of his days in the South Seas:

> Here he lies where he longed to be;
> Home is the sailor, home from the sea,
> And the hunter home from the hill.

So of Coleridge's chance remark that our terrestrial navigation has to depend on celestial observations. So of Chesterton's lines in his Christmas poem:

> And they lay their heads in a foreign land
> Whenever the day is done.

So of John Tauler's saying that "it is God who is at home, and we who are in the far country." So of Carlyle's apostrophe to the whole history of mankind, "Generation after generation emerges from the Inane, hastes stormfully across the astonished earth and plunges again into the Inane. But whence, O Heaven whither? Sense knows not, Faith knows not, only that it is through Mystery to Mystery, from God and to God."

Josiah Royce, our one-time colleague here, was not a very orthodox churchman, but so, also, Royce in his sober appraisal of our religion, "Christianity stands before us as the most effective expression of religious longing which the human race, travailing in pain until now, has endeavored to translate by the labor of love into the terms of its own real life. Christianity is, thus far, man's most impressive vision of salvation and his principal glimpse of the homeland of the spirit."

It is very hard to disparage and dismiss convictions such as these, which are a deep and native part of the human mind and heart. But if they all seem merely fanciful poetry or speculative philosophy, let me end these random quotations with a single sentence written by Bishop Barry. They seem to me to fit our troubled times: "For us the world is no longer a home. For in order to be at home in this world it is not unfortunately sufficient to disbelieve in another."

The great danger of any observation of Easter is that it may be the one day in the year we come to church and the one day in the year when we think about these things. The danger is that, as the day may be an exception in our lives, we shall think of it as having been an exception in its own day. In a sense Easter always seems to come too soon after Good Friday. It asks too radical a change in our thought and our feelings. But in so far as we believe that the total record falls within the realm of history rather than of legend, we tend to think of the recorded fact as a mysterious miracle which happened once to Christ but never again to anyone else.

It is for this reason that I suggested as a text those words from the cross: "Father, into thy hands I commend my spirit." That cry is the liaison between these two very disparate days, Good Friday and Easter, and makes them part of a single consistent life. Whatever else Jesus believed, he believed that he came from God and went to God; that God is the God of the living and not of the dead; that it is life which matters, life more abundant; that he has pioneered for us all and that where he is, there shall we be also.

The whole idea of our immortality is not primarily a matter of the indefinite prolongation of our life in time. As has been, so is—this is the Buddhist idea of hell and not of heaven. Our meditations on the matter must always be translated into the terms of what St. John's Gospel calls "eternal life." Eternal life is not merely life in time, it is a quality of life, a different kind of life from that we know only too well. It is this prospect and this faith that touches the human heart and stirs the human mind. As the old woman in Synge's play says, "I have put away sorrow like a shoe that is muddy and worn out."

What draws us to Christ at Easter time is not merely the ongoing life into which he entered after the cross, but the eternal life which he lived while here. That eternal life was uninterruptedly lived in the loving thought of God, his Father. We must believe that he lives on in God, not because of a sudden miracle wrought in him, but by virtue of the very indestructibility of his filial devotion to God which, in the line of the hymn, was "the passion of his life those three and thirty years." If anything in all this world deserves to endure it is the mind and heart of Christ. Nothing else can be as indestructible as that. Therefore, our daily answer to Job's question ought to be a practice of eternal life. We do not have to wait for that. We may pass even here and now from death into life.

It is doubtful whether any one of us is an entire stranger to some experience of what is meant by eternal life. Such moments, which are self-explanatory and self-sufficient, come to us like the wind blowing where it listeth. They may come when we dare to rest on the world of nature, or in the hours of friendship and affection. They may come in church, but they are certainly not guaranteed by the church. They may come with some great work of art. What we feel about them is that in their own right they will last always. The world cannot take them away because what we know as the world did not give them. Those of us who sang and shared in singing the St. John Passion, and many who listened, ought to understand what St. John's Gospel means by eternal life.

> The same old baffling questions. O my friend,
> I cannot answer them. In vain I send
> My soul into the dark, where never burn
> The lamps of science, nor the natural light
> Of reason's sun and stars. . . .
>
> I have no answer for myself or thee,
> Save that I learned beside my mother's knee,
> "All is of God that is, and is to be,
> And God is good." Let this suffice us still,
> Resting in childlike trust upon His will,
> Who moves to his great end, unthwarted by the ill.

XXI

I GO A FISHING
A Sermon for the Sunday after Easter

Text: Simon Peter saith unto them; I go a fishing.—JOHN 21:3

THESE simple words are one of the most moving sayings in all the Bible. But one must stop and think *who* said them and *when,* and *why* he said them. The fishing that he was going to do was not, as it had once been, a matter of a livelihood and the day's work. His going a fishing was a confession of utter disillusionment.

Many of the twelve apostles are little more than names. For the purposes of Christian art they are lay figures to fill niches on the west front of a cathedral. They are neutral, lifeless, and without character.

There was, however, one man among them who never fails to come alive. That man is Simon Peter. Coleridge once said that he knew that the Bible was true because it found him. We know that Peter is true because he finds us. He was human-all-too-human. He was generous, impulsive, a man of both faith

172

and doubt. On one memorable night he denied his Lord, only to go out and weep bitterly at what he had done.

This was the man who said, "I go a fishing." He was back again by the Sea of Galilee. For the sake of his Lord and Master, who had once come there and called him, he had left his father and the boats and the nets to follow that Master. He followed him, as the days passed into weeks, the weeks into months, and perhaps the months into years. We do not know how long. Over all that time following Jesus was the only life that Simon Peter knew. It was he who hazarded the bold guess that Jesus was the Messiah. From that moment on he followed in bewilderment and in a kind of blind trust— often he followed afar off. He followed Jesus up to Jerusalem, to be with him when the Kingdom should come, to sit beside him on the throne, to share in the final fulfillment of a thousand years of waiting and hoping.

Then things went wrong. Jesus gathered the twelve around him and spoke of his dying rather than of his reigning. He was betrayed by one of them. He was tried and condemned and crucified. Schweitzer says that perhaps, even for Jesus himself, his hopes for his Messianic Kingdom fell in upon his head with those words from the cross, "My God, my God, why hast thou forsaken me?" However it may have been with Jesus, this was certainly true for his followers. Most of them fled before the end. They made their way back to Galilee. It is there that we find them, in this lovely story in St. John's Gospel, a story which is like a thin veil between two worlds. We do not need to press it too hard for fact; its truth is that of poetry.

One can see this little band of disappointed and disillusioned men back by the lakeside once more. They were silent and motionless, waiting for someone to speak, waiting for the one most likely man of all to say something. Finally he did speak, and what he said was simply this, "I go a fishing. They say unto him, We also go with thee."

Those four words of Peter carry with them an almost insufferable freight of bitterness and sorrow, all the regret of which the human mind and heart are capable. How could things which had promised so much have gone so wrong? How could one who had always seemed so sure of himself have been so mistaken as to himself? Why had they ever scorched their understanding at his flaming brow? Could they ever trust another man again? Could they ever trust themselves again? All that was left of the best that the world had offered men for generations was the cold ashes of a fire that had gone out.

Probably they had been fools in the first place, ever to leave the one thing they knew and could do well—their fishing on the Sea of Galilee. They ought to have known better than to have followed that fanatic. They should have turned him a deaf ear at the first, and sent him away on his own fool's errand. If Peter had in him a streak of the idealist, he had also and always an iron vein of realism. So it was this vein of realism that now came to his rescue. We may charge the man with inconsistency, with most of the frailties to which our flesh is liable. But we cannot charge him with sentimentalism. He would go back to the world he knew well, to the world in which he could handle himself and his affairs. He would take up his life where he had dropped it, and try to forget all that had happened in the meantime. "Simon Peter saith unto them, I go a fishing. They say unto him, We also go with thee."

As the story goes on we read that they went forth and entered a ship immediately, and that night they caught nothing. Had they lost the knack of it? Had they forgotten how to fish? Plainly it was not going to be as simple and as easy as they had thought, to solve their problem by going back to their fishing.

And then—"When the morning was now come, Jesus stood on the shore. . . . Therefore that disciple whom Jesus loved saith unto Peter, It is the Lord. Now when Simon Peter heard that it was the Lord, he girt his fisher's coat unto him, . . . and did cast himself into the sea. . . . Jesus saith to Simon Peter, Simon, son of Jonas, lovest thou me more than these? He saith unto him, Yea, Lord; thou knowest that I love thee. . . . Jesus saith unto him, . . . follow thou me." The very words that had been said there, at the first.

One thing is quite clear about the stories of the resurrection of Christ. However we interpret them this is plain. Something happened to change a frightened little company of stunned and disillusioned fishermen into the hard enduring core of the Christian Church. The appearances of Christ had for them, as they must have for us, the hallmark of spiritual reality. Otherwise the origins of Christianity are inexplicable and even irrational.

Meanwhile, of all the stories of Easter and of the days that followed, this of Simon Peter's fishing is in some ways the one that comes nearest to the circumstances and need of our own time.

Those of us who hark back to the years before World War I

used to follow Christian spokesmen who promised us that the Kingdom of God should soon appear. There can have been few generations between the first century and this twentieth century that have suffered such disillusionment or have seen their eager hopes so long deferred.

I listened not long ago to Alan Valentine, then president of the University of Rochester, unexpectedly baring his mind and heart to a little company of his faculty. He said he was a moral and spiritual casualty of World War I, that he fought through that war only to be disillusioned. Its failure to achieve what it promised had scarred and embittered his whole life. He had gone on doing his work but had never really dared again to give himself unreservedly to bold ideals.

Shortly after World War II a letter came to me from England, saying, "Most people one meets are awfully depressed and fed up. For the first time I feel that life on this island is getting drab, monotonous and depressing. And the world news and the lack of the will to peace don't make you want to say, Well all this is worth while, for the sake of the future."

There is no need to labor the point. We Americans are, in material things, far better off than most of our contemporaries the world around. Whether we are any better off morally or spiritually is another matter. The transgression against the Holy Spirit is always that of cynicism. If one wants to put it in the terms of Peter's denial of his Lord, the sin of treason. There may be a few immune souls who are defended by nature or by grace from this sin. But for most persons this has been, and still is, the essence of all that is meant by being tempted of the Devil.

It is out of the recurring disappointments and delays and evasions of all these latter years that there arises the menace of the mood of Simon Peter of so long ago—and we can almost overhear ourselves saying, "I go a fishing." I will be a realist, I will have done with faith and hope and love. He who has never felt the seduction of this sin against the Holy Spirit is an exceptional person. Whether he is really a fortunate person, who is to be congratulated, I am not sure. For it has been said, "He ascended into heaven means nothing in want of the prior words, He descended into hell."

There is, however, one thing that may be safely prophesied of our attempt to go a fishing. It will not be as simple a solution of our personal problems as we may think. Remember that those fishermen of long ago fished all night and caught nothing. The waters of bitter realism will not yield us much of a livelihood. No civilized man has ever really succeeded in going native in some primitive society. He can never wholly slough off the self he brings with him. So no man, who has ever given himself to any loyalty or cause or ideal, can rid himself thereafter of those commitments. If he tries to deny them they haunt him. If he says "I never knew them" the cock will crow thrice and he will find himself going out and weeping bitterly.

If one has ever been an idealist, a believer, his ideals and his faith live on with him forever after, if not to inspire him, then to reproach him and to recall him and to redeem him. The most obvious solution of one's personal doubts and perplexities may well be to "go a fishing." But that will not prove anything. Once one has believed and hoped one has put oneself beyond being saved by that kind of evasion and escape. One is imputing to realism meanings and resources which it can never have. It might have served one well before one followed one's cause or one's Christ. But it cannot serve one now as it served one then. It is no answer to the imperatives of our time, to the fightings without and the fears within, to say, "I go a fishing."

The story of the resurrection appearances of Christ to his disciples on Easter Day is the sort of record that a spiritual order requires. Even if it were lacking in the Gospels we should feel that we must re-create something of the sort to fulfill the fact. Either our world is reasonable and spiritual, or else it is ultimately meaningless. If Christ Jesus was killed once for all, and that was the end of the matter for him, and thus for us, then much of what we mean by the world of the spirit is simply an interim solace and sustenance.

So, when they said, "It is the Lord," they were witnessing in those words to all that we mean by a spiritual realm, and by Christianity. The figure of Christ standing there by the lakeside becomes for us a guarantee of the indestructibleness, the permanence, the eternal life in our own experience of all our own sincere devotions and ideals. We may think the world can destroy them, or that we ourselves can deny them finally. But we are wrong. There is about every honest and loyal act of ours, however imperfectly we may have redeemed it, an intimation of immortality. We think that we can disassemble the world of our devotions because we have invented them. We are wrong. We do not invent them. We did not call Christ to join us; he called us to follow him. We do not choose him; he has chosen us. We do not apprehend him; he apprehends us. Most of the greater events of life have about them this quality, not of our own planning, but of some mysterious outer compulsion. "I felt," said Kelvin, "as I was drawing near the truth that the truth was also drawing near to me." So the Christian will say, I felt not that I was drawing near to Christ, but that Christ was drawing near to me.

> Say not the struggle naught availeth,
> The labor and the wounds are vain, . . .
> . . . .
> For while the tired waves, vainly breaking,
> Seem here no painful inch to gain,
> Far back, through creeks and inlets making,
> Comes silent, flooding in, the main.

That, and much more than that, is implicit in those far-off words, "It is the Lord." There is no faith that the world needs more this Easter time than that. It is not, of itself, a mechanical solution of the problems we face. It does not tell us how much money to give to Greece or how far to go into Turkey. But this faith is the inward nature of the serenity and security of the life of the Christian. It is the secret of that central peace subsisting at the heart of endless agitation.

One word more. I have often been trying to say that the religious problem of our day is whether our humanity is alone with itself, or whether there is some correspondence between our imperfect human efforts and that Eternal Goodness which we believe to be the heart of the universe. I am more and more persuaded that the ever-debated question of the immortality of man is not that of some hypothetical projection of our imperfect human experience into other areas where it may have still further chances to perfect itself. Not that: But rather our wandering humanity saying, "I will arise and go to my Father." Rather his disciples saying with the Christ, "I go to my Father and to your Father."

We are confronted today by more than thirty years that have seen lives cut short, mangled, saddened, frustrated in the terms of their threescore years and ten. All around us in the wider world there is still famine, misery, battle, murder and sudden death. It ought not to be beneath the intellectual self-respect of any thoughtful person to say, "Earth hath no sorrows that heaven cannot heal." This is not a matter of a cheap and easy answer to a hard problem. It is a matter of the integrity of a moral and spiritual order. It is our Christian right and privilege on Easter Day to commend any one such person, and each of such, "to the bosom of his Father and his God."

XXII

LIVING IN DIFFICULT TIMES
A Commencement Sermon

Text: A great door and effectual is opened unto me, and there are many adversaries.—I CORINTHIANS 16:9

WE are familiar with the map of the United States. Along our northern boundary is the chain of the Great Lakes. They are connected by narrow rivers and rapids and falls.

It is a relatively simple matter for a ship to make her way across one or another of the Lakes. It is a more difficult business to negotiate the straits which lie between the Lakes. Channels are narrow, traffic is heavy, currents are swift. At times shipping must be handled through a succession of locks from one level to another.

Most human lives are rather like that. There are broad and open periods of relatively quiet times. Then there are brief periods of rapid transition from one pattern of life to another.

The tranquil years present few difficulties. At such times life is self-explanatory and more or less self-sufficient.

But all of us are likely to run into trouble—emotional, psychological and moral trouble—in the sudden and swift periods of radical change. We do not quite know how to handle ourselves when we find that we are moving out of some serene and familiar stretch of years into an unknown future. Leaving home and going to college is such an experience. Leaving college and going on to graduate study or out into the world is another. Getting married, making a home, the coming of a first child, the loss of a job, facing an unexpected illness, the death of someone near to us and dear. All these are the rapids of a human life. They are the times for which we are unprepared, when we are only too liable to make a mess of our lives. We cannot ever imagine them fully in advance, but at least we should know that in the order of nature they must come to us. I have ventured to say these things because, whether you like it or not, you are in these three or four days passing out of one of your Great Lakes into the rapids of graduation from college. In some ways this is one of the most radical transits you will ever have to make. You cannot go on pretending hereafter that you are still an undergraduate. Much of your happiness in years to come is going to depend upon the skill with which you negotiate the next few weeks and months.

Beyond these intimate matters I have in mind the whole pattern of history and the nature of these years in which all of us together are involved. For the life of society as a whole, like the life of the individual, seems to involve a succession of contrasted experiences. There are broad and wide and relatively tranquil stretches of years covering the lifetime of a whole generation, sometimes of a succession of generations. Then there are short periods of swift and radical change which alter the whole pattern of social life. One's expectation of life and indeed the whole manner of one's living depend upon a right appraisal of the kind of time in which one is living.

There is no doubt as to the kind of time through which we are now living. We are living in one of the periods of rapid change in history. This period began with the onset of World War I. It has been in process for all the intervening years, and no one can hazard a guess as to how much longer it will go on, or when and how we shall come out into more open and quiet waters.

Meanwhile, our happiness and our effectiveness depend upon our making our mental peace with this fact. By making our mental peace with the fact of a fast-changing world I do not mean necessarily liking it, or approving of it, or thinking of it as final, much less being broken and defeated by it. But I do mean accepting it as a fact. For no one can do anything with hard facts who tries to pretend that they are not there.

There are, of course, alternatives which weak or timid natures elect. There is the ivory tower of the dilettante, there are the romantic fantasies of the mentally unstable, there are the escape mechanisms of the coward, and there is the settled cynicism of the disillusioned. These are all well-known devices for dodging hard facts, but if one resorts to them in days such as ours, we can only say that in so doing one drops out of the real life of the times and becomes a social anachronism.

Therefore, making your mental peace in advance with the kind of world into which you are now going is a necessity. Your ability to do so will be the measure of your education, and of your morals and ultimately of your religion. All other forms of lesser personal peace will depend upon the existence of this prior and major peace. Wordsworth, who also lived through a revolutionary time in history, called it "central peace, subsisting at the heart of endless agitation."

It would be hard to find a better account of the frame of mind by which we achieve that kind of peace than the verse from St. Paul which is our text for the afternoon: "A great door and effectual is opened unto me, and there are many adversaries." There are great opportunities and there are real difficulties.

The passkey to the verse lies in the striking use made of the word "and." For, left to himself and without resolution of mind, the average person would say 'but" instead of "and." "A great door and effectual is opened unto me, *but* there are many difficulties." St. Paul, however, did not say "but"; he said "and." It is the difference between the runner in a hurdle race who stubs his toe at every hurdle, thus slowing himself down at every jump, and the runner who takes the hurdle in his stride without tripping over it. For if the runner says to himself, "I have a chance to run and perhaps to win this race, but there are many hurdles in the way," he has cut the nerve of effort at once. His eye is on the hurdles rather than on the finish line, and they have already defeated him. If we are to run life's race successfully today we must learn how to take its obstacles in our stride.

Let me mention two or three of the obstacles which we have to learn to take in our stride. Each of us is, in the first instance, his own worst enemy. The anonymous medieval mystic who wrote the *Theologia Germanica* said, "All deception beginneth in self-deception." The amount of self-deception which we all allow ourselves, sometimes unconscious and sometimes conscious, is far greater than we realize. To know oneself and then to accept the truth about oneself is a hard task. Our deep-rooted capacity for self-deception is one of the most common causes for our unhappiness and our failures at living. So one harks back to the words of the old monk in *The Brothers Karamazov* speaking to the young novice, "This above all; don't lie to yourself."

Then, we in America ought to be on our guard against the insidious influence of the massive materialism of our country in our day. We are not a bad or cruel people. When he left here George Santayana paid us the compliment of saying that if he looked in the heart of a man and did not find kindness there he would know he was not an American. But our yardsticks are patterned to measure things rather than ideas. If one takes the blatant advertising in our journals as such a yardstick one would never suppose that we have minds, let alone souls. The main appeal is to the care and comfort and glorification of our bodies.

A hundred years ago Henry Thoreau sat on the edge of Walden Pond and watched the linemen putting up wires along the tracks of the Fitchburg Railway. "We are," he said, "in great haste to construct a magnetic telegraph from Maine to Texas; but Maine and Texas it may be have nothing important to communicate. . . . Our inventions are but improved means to an unimproved end." His words are more true today than they were then. A relief worker in Central Europe says that we ought to realize that there are people there who would rather have an encyclopedia than a television set or a deep freeze.

Then there is the contagious seduction of the mass movements of our time. They invite us to unload the responsibilities of personal life upon society as a whole. If we will only become fellow travelers we can hand over the direction of our lives to some dictator. Thoreau's neighbor Emerson once said, "We see young people who owe us a new world so bravely do they promise, but they either die young or else they dodge the account and are lost in the crowd." The temptation to lose oneself in the crowd is very great today.

Well, we can think of our hurdles for ourselves. But whatever they are, the point is to recognize them as such, to admit they are difficult to negotiate and nevertheless to take them in our stride.

For if we can say with St. Paul, "And there are many adversaries," they are in a certain sense the actual measure of our opportunities.

So it is that Bishop Stubbs, one of the distinguished English historians of the last generation, said of his published work that it had always had to be written under difficult conditions. He was hurried, other duties pressed upon him, he had to deliver a speech or a manuscript on a given day. He dreamed of a time when he should have leisure and quiet and ideal conditions for writing. Yet he found himself wondering whether, if he had such conditions, he would do even as good work as he had done. He came to the conclusion that our best work is usually done "against the grain." That is a reassuring word for us today since we, too, are having to do much of our work against the grain of what may seem to be an unideal time.

Yet in spite of this fact a great door and effectual is opened, a genuine opportunity awaits us, if only we learn to take the intervening difficulties in our stride. We have a chance to make homes that can stand the wear and tear of daily life. We can take our part in teaching the oncoming generation. We can share in the social services of our time. The best of us can actually pioneer in one or another of the sciences at the place where the bow of the ship cuts into uncharted waters. Some of us may be drafted by church or state for the difficult and engrossing tasks of reconstruction in war-stricken lands. There are open doors enough and necessary work to be done if only we will look beyond, and thus overlook, the intervening difficulties. Let me quote in closing, as a footnote to our text, an inscription on the walls of the Chapel of Staunton Harold in Leicestershire:

IN THE YEAR 1653

WHEN ALL THINGS SACRED WERE

EITHER DEMOLISHED OR PROFANED

SIR ROBERT SHIRLEY, BARONET,

FOUNDED THIS CHURCH:

WHOSE SINGULAR PRAISE IT IS

TO HAVE DONE THE BEST THINGS IN THE

WORST TIMES AND

HOPED THEM IN THE MOST CALAMITOUS

It will be a reasonably easy thing for you to live, from now on, an undistinguished life. Whatever distinction you achieve and whatever praise you are to deserve will follow the fact that you will have "done the best things in the worst times and hoped them in the most calamitous."

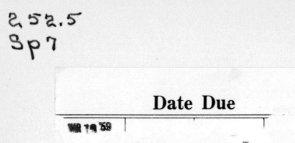